The Lost Chords

The Lost Chords

Reginald Frary

CANTERBURY
PRESS
Norwich

© Reginald Frary 2009

First published in 2009 by the Canterbury Press Norwich
Editorial office
13–17 Long Lane,
London, EC1A 9PN, UK

Canterbury Press is an imprint of Hymns Ancient
and Modern Ltd (a registered charity)
St Mary's Works, St Mary's Plain,
Norwich, NR3 3BH, UK

www.scm-canterburypress.co.uk

British Library Cataloguing in Publication data

A catalogue record for this book is available
from the British Library

978-1-85311-977-4

Printed and bound in Great Britain by
CPI Bookmarque, Croydon, CR0 4TD

Contents

Preface

In my early choirboy days the concept was vaguely puzzling to me. Later, with the experiences of working under the direction of a colourful collection of choirmasters and organists, I became more puzzled – How and why did the idea of heavenly choirs singing night and day, non-stop for ever and ever, become so very attractive to generations of hymn writers? I wondered if any of them had ever actually sung in their local church choirs. In my choir we enjoyed singing all right but sometimes when we eventually reached the end of a long drawn out, chaotic choir practice conducted by a bad tempered choirmaster who'd just had a steaming row with the vicar over the introduction of a new hymn tune and considered us all unmusical morons because we couldn't seem to get the hang of it, we were only too delighted to escape. Mercifully, the outrageous thought of the singing continuing beyond nine o'clock Friday evening and carrying on for ever and ever never entered our minds as we sped from the vestry.

I have sometimes wondered, however, whether that thought may have found favour with one of our choirmasters who always found the greatest difficulty in closing choir practice at 9 o'clock and on Sundays, carried on the Evensong organ voluntary long after everyone in the congregation and choir had left the church and the vicar had locked up and gone home…

R. F.

1

Trams and Choirboys

It was to be, I suppose, how our conversation developed from mutual admiration and endorsement of the most environmentally friendly – and most unjustly ignored – public transport road vehicle, the tram. We were strangers to each other, travelling on a modern tram near Wimbledon and were obviously both enjoying the ride with 1930s schoolboy enthusiasm. We got talking. 'Yes', Tim, who was in Town on business, told me, 'as long as I can remember I've doted on trams. When I was a kid living in London I always wanted to drive one. They were the old double-deckers in those days and my favourite enjoyment was to ride down Tulse Hill in a rolling, rattling, devil-may-care veteran of the tracks with a lovely clanging bell and a large blue enamel "Don't Spit" notice at the top of the iron stairway. I was a choirboy from a very early age and for me the great thing about *being* a choirboy was that I travelled to church all by myself three times a week at the front of the top deck of a tram.' He beamed at the memory. 'Well, I'm still a choir person but in a much smaller choir than I knew as a boy. We just can't get the choirboys now, which means we're hard up for tenors and basses for the future. And sadly, for me, there are no trams within miles to ride to church on – nothing on rails at all, in fact. Years ago that man, Beeching, even cut off our local train link so we all go about now in big gas-guzzling, polluting cars and my wife gets real mad at me always moaning about no choirboys and no trams.'

When Tim learned that I also was a long-term chorister as well as a tram man and shared his views completely about the shameful lack of trams and choirboys, he said we must keep in touch on these matters and I agreed enthusiastically as our tram reached the depot and its lovely sounding bell clanged back the years for us.

A few weeks later we were in touch again by email (his wife was overjoyed that he'd found someone apart from her to moan to about the choirboy and tram dilemma) and he'd caught my firm attention with his accounts of the musical goings-on in his parish. 'We have no choirboys,' he confirmed regretfully, 'but we do have our Sunday School superintendent who was a conductress on London trams in her very early years.'

So Tim started to tell me his latest choir story and the emails came thick and fast…

The old vicar of Tim's country town parish church (part awe-inspiring pure Medieval, part through-the-centuries local builders' bodge-up) greatly appreciates the choir because they sing everything, whatever it is, at enthusiastic full blast – words of meditation, phrases of sadness and remorse, gentle children's verses, victorious battle cries, all roar forth from the choir and carry the service along at a spanking, breakneck pace, and not one of the singers ever glares at the old vicar when he joins them with his huge, football hooligan tones. Indeed, they welcome his contribution towards ensuring that any sluggish, quavering voices in the congregation that could slow down the headlong pace of the choir are obliterated and the service finishes bang on time so that the choir are never late for their traditional Sunday get-together at The Red Cow (an establishment referred to in private by the super aloof vicar's warden as a low tavern for low persons).

Until recently, it was a very different matter for the old vicar when he conducted an occasional service at the parish's daughter church (distinguished early Georgian architect, special elevated pews for the mayor and corporation and handsomely intrusive monuments to the local departed elite), a very superior establishment which even in these days of congregational togetherness is still often distantly referred to as 'the posh church' and 'carriage trade'. In keeping with its status it boasts a superb choir who, unlike the parish church choir, *never* welcome the old vicar's vocal contribution as he shatters their peerless performances with his jolly parish church bellowing.

'On the whole, though,' Tim told me, 'the old vicar is popular, indeed well-loved, throughout the parish and his modern young curate who runs the daughter church for him does fully realize that the old man *is* vicar of both churches, so on the occasions when the old vicar conducts a service at the superior daughter church nowadays the superb choir do their best, as a special favour to make him feel at home, by keeping their Vivaldi, Bach and Purcell offerings well out of the way and substituting a congregational selection – a virtual battery of the old vicar's favourite warlike Victorian hymns all about mighty armies, slaying hoards of the wicked and Satan's hosts fleeing and angel choirs singing in celebration without end. Then the whole affair is climaxed by the organist pulling all the stops and blasting everyone out of church with the "Colonel Bogey" march, after which the organist and choir of the superior daughter church stay still for a few moments quietly wondering how on earth they have brought themselves to take part in this demonstration of debased Victorian sentimentality and brute force and ignorance just for the old vicar's sake.'

I opined that the old vicar must indeed be *extremely* well-loved by the superb choir and organist for them to get mixed up with all that sentimentality and ignorance. 'Is it because the vicar is old?' I asked.

'Well, that's the funny thing,' mused Tim. 'He's not really old at all – just approaching early middle age. I think the "old" label has stuck because he still wears a proper clerical collar at all times – not just a sliver of white plastic shoved on under his chin a moment or two before the service begins …'

Tim sent me an umpteenth email. 'I wonder if you'd like to take a Sunday off from your church and come down here for a singing experience you'll never forget?' he invited. 'On Sunday week we have our patronal festival (it's all to do with togetherness between our two churches really – the vicar reckons there must be more togetherness) and we're doing a sort of "hymn sandwich" service with *both* choirs and congregations present. I won't say *combined* choirs because we've got different ideas of how to sing things and we go our separate ways. It saves a lot of argument.'

I arrived at Tim's church, early and eager, on a bright July Sunday morning and Tim, already robed in a flamboyant, in fact startling, crimson cassock, met me at the vestry door. Also, around the doorway there were a fussily moving crowd of people carrying choir robes and music and looking rather cross, I thought. They appeared to be attempting to enter the vestry past a vast red-faced gentleman also, like Tim, wearing a flamboyant cassock, who kept on announcing boisterously 'Not in 'ere – in the 'all'.

'He's our bass soloist,' explained Tim, 'and all those people milling around him are the superb choir from our daughter church. This kind of thing happens whenever we have a combined patronal service. They *always* make straight for our vestry to rehearse their music – to get the light and shade right. I don't know why they bother because our parish church choir don't go in much for light and shade – we go for a more full-blooded effort, y'see, and so the congregation don't really hear their light bits anyway.'

'But there's no harm in letting them into the vestry to practise, is there?' I reasoned.

'Oh, we can't have that,' explained Tim. 'We've got the special patronal festival darts match at The Red Cow straight after the service this morning and our choir are brushing up their tactics in our vestry. We always do. It's traditional.'

'Round here, round here, ladies and gentlemen.' Tim took over from the big bass and the cross-looking superb choir followed him into the Sunday School room. They trailed in under the eye of the Sunday School superintendent who looked like a frail, genteel, very sweet old lady, but was, as Tim assured me under his breath, actually a thoroughly seasoned, hard-as-iron old warrior of the

Victorian school, she indeed whose crowd controlling expertise had been schooled and matured as a conductress keeping the passengers in order on board the last of London's historic trams. A woman loved and feared by all. 'Come along! Come along!' she commanded one or two bewildered-looking superb choir stragglers. 'My pupils will be here at any moment – they'd better be! – so,' turning the sweet old lady mask directly on to the choir master, 'do your rehearsing and get your lot into the choir stalls, sharp. Right! Off you go then, no time to waste!' (Tim told me later that he sometimes speculated on how she managed the togetherness on her tram just after a big Saturday football match when the home team had lost.)

Spending much time rehearsing in the presence of the tram-conducting martinet didn't really appeal to the superb choir or their organist and in no time they shuffled confusedly into their reserved choir stalls. 'Every year it's like this,' Tim explained. 'Their choir become sort of uneasy when they come here, sort of bewildered, sort of ...'

'Shattered,' I suggested.

'Yes, exactly,' he agreed, '"shattered." The lady does seem to have that sort of effect on all grown ups. Her Sunday School kids take no notice of her, of course.'

Once in the choir stalls the superb choir soon recovered as their organist started to speak quietly to them. 'There he goes,' said Tim. 'He's trying to boost their confidence, y'see. He's telling them to be sure they take no notice of our choir's singing because it could get them into bad habits.'

And so, the patronal festival combined service went off very well with the parish church choir and the superb

6

choir facing each other across the chancel and singing the same hymns at roughly (sometimes very roughly) the same time, although, as the service proceeded the superb choir did appear to be becoming rather more bewildered by the noise and the parish church choir more loudly inspired by the sounds of the old vicar's choice of fighting-spirit hymns.

The vicar delivered a more than usually fervent sermon on the joys of togetherness (although by some oversight he failed to mention that the saint the patronal festival service was supposed to be all about was a hermit) and members of the two congregations eyed each other quite pleasantly at the following stand-up lunch in the church hall.

Having dealt firmly with the Sunday School pupils' usual appalling lack of biblical knowledge, the once feared superintendent conducted them into the church hall through the mass of congregation members who were standing chatting (mostly just standing) right across the narrow entrance. 'Pass along the car,' she ordered and everyone did.

All agreed that the combined patronal festival service had been a worthwhile togetherness experience, particularly the musical presentation. Parishioners agreed they'd never heard anything quite like it. Nevertheless, the organist-conductor of the superb choir didn't stay around to join in any more togetherness. He cycled quietly back to the daughter church, climbed into the organ loft and, in the blissful peace of that empty place, took out his packet of cheese and tomato sandwiches and munched contentedly.

2

The Dream of the New Lady Curate

The small church of St John, comfortably established in rural southern England 150 years ago, where my friend George has been a member of the choir for longer than he can remember, is a typical nineteenth-century Gothic temple that was pleasing to the eye of most of its Victorian churchgoers (and even those who only knew it as a horse-bus stop), lending a gentle dignity to the neighbourhood and an atmosphere of general well-being.

Nowadays, sadly, it is difficult for this church to lend any kind of atmosphere because, unless you know where it is and you are standing very close to it, it's hardly possible to detect it amidst the encroaching chaos of the threatening black glass tower block, sprawling garish supermarket and brutal, monster multi-storey car park.

However, there are a considerable number of local residents who do know it's still there and it is quite well supported by congregation, choir and bell ringers. In traditional fashion, these individual sections of the worshippers don't normally see eye to eye about the running of their church, except, of course, at the parish bumper Christmas party when everybody agrees with everyone else and smiles, hugs and shakes hands and the vicar is heartened and encouraged to carry on for another year.

The vicar is known as a nice man – one of those always referred to in parish magazines as 'loved by all' when they move to another parish or, at long last, retire. On Sunday mornings, before the service, this nice vicar invariably slaps you on the back and beams 'Jolly good! Splendid! Great!' even though you've only just arrived at church and haven't done anything in particular on which to be congratulated apart, perhaps, from resisting the temptation of staying in bed for an extra hour.

The organist (a doctor of music and therefore referred to as 'the Doc'), who is also the choirmaster, thoroughly enjoys Sundays at the church. He likes to feel that he is regarded as a martinet, an absolute ruler of an all embracing autocratic set-up – his choir. He's one of *that* sort (power mad, George says). He has a habit of clicking his heels and standing to attention, staring above their heads when greeting ladies, particularly lady altos who he doesn't like because, he says, they are pushy and not as good as male altos who he can't find these days.

He appears to slightly modify his iron attitude to the choirboys ('you stupid urchins, I don't know why I even bother with you at all. Now, sing it again without draping yourselves all over the choir stalls') only when the soprano soloist, a delightful girl with red hair and a glorious voice, tells him to shut up bullying or she won't sing 'Oh for the wings of a dove' at his birthday Evensong.

My friend George is the oldest and longest serving member of the choir and the Doc keeps on arranging presentations to celebrate his record. To date he has two chiming clocks, a toaster, an electric lawn mower and a magnificent studded collar for his pet mastiff. George is very touched by the Doc's thoughtfulness but the beautiful red-haired soprano reckons the Doc is only doing all this to remind George that he and his voice have been in this choir quite long enough and they should retire and give the rest of the choir a chance to sing a hymn actually in tune. That George doesn't take the hint but simply carries on cheerfully accepting the awards and singing flat is a minor irritation to the Doc, as is the nice vicar's constant gentle efforts in trying to draw the choir out of their rather enclosed musical world and into the joy of full parish fellowship. In this, members can join in bravely helping out in the youth club (a sort of policing job) or the Sunday School, or making sure the churchyard doesn't run completely wild, occasionally risking life and limb attempting to clean the church's almost unreachable clerestory windows or atop a swaying ladder replacing light bulbs in remote regions of the soaring chancel arch. And, of course, there is always the opportunity of attending the special annual committee meeting, concerned solely with the absorbing question of whether the church's superb oak pews should be ripped out and replaced with nice, brightly coloured plastic chairs.

Then, recently, a rather more than minor irritation for the Doc had come about in the arrival in the parish of an extraordinarily forceful part-time lady curate. George says she is a tax official during the week but now wants to get away from such sordid matters and think higher thoughts during the weekends. The part-time young woman's higher thoughts have already alerted the choir. It turns out that she doesn't like Victorian hymns and 'old-fashioned' choirs in old-fashioned robes. She herself doesn't wear a clerical collar but merely slips a sliver of white plastic under her chin just before the service. She has already strongly recommended that the choir should come down from their lofty perches in the choir stalls and sing among the congregation – 'and I beg of you fervently not the awful sentimental puerile Victorian stuff that some choirs unfortunately still do sing!'

The nice vicar who always endeavours, sometimes desperately, to agree with everyone had said that having the choir in a nice friendly fashion sitting among the congregation would be a really jolly idea but he'd made it clear that the idea was actually not his – since being urgently warned by his wife that if the new lady curate tried to push through her ideas, the whole choir and the Doc would go straight down the road and join the much larger parish church choir who sang even more awful sentimental puerile hymns than at St John's. Further, the veteran parish church organist now wanted to retire, thus leaving the coast clear for the absolute ruler of St John's to forcefully offer his musical services for the vacant post and, of course, being successful, proceed to drum into the parish church choir just how to really perform awful sentimental, puerile Victorian music.

'Everything here is in a state of flux with all these disruptive influences threatening the traditional peace of the parish', wrote George in a letter inviting me to be a guest in the choir on the approaching occasion of the Doc's birthday Evensong where traditionally 'Oh for the wings of a dove' was sung by the choir's delightful red-haired soprano soloist. George told me when we met later that the holding of the service had been going on for years – it's truly traditional. So they hadn't always had the same soloist of course, he said. The one before this one had had a truly sensational voice, he acknowledged in awed tones. 'But she was a true battle-axe type, nobody in the choir could stand her.' He noticed my look of surprise. 'Well, you know how it is. These people suddenly realize they can sing a bit and they have some lessons and get above themselves – and the vicar never stops slapping them on the back and bawling "Jolly good! Splendid! Great!" So what can you expect?'

'But the present soloist is all right?' I said.

George spoke warmly. 'Well, she's one of us. Her dad's a bass who can shake the foundations of the church when he gets going and her grandfather used to pump the organ by hand, when he was a choirboy – anyway, see you Sunday.'

I arrived good and early at George's church on the Sunday of the Doc's special birthday Evensong service and George took me straight into the choir vestry which appeared to be somewhere under the organ, reached through a sort of cellar filled with various ladders, buckets and gardening equipment and a large black-framed sepia photo of a bearded Victorian vicar who looked rather annoyed, I thought. George said the choir had been put down here in the bowels of the earth some 50 years ago because when the choir vestry was on the ground floor the congregation used to complain that the noise of last-minute rehearsals just before the service upset their quiet meditative moments. They could cope with the noise of the choir during the service, but expecting them to put up with it before the service as well was a bit much.

George opened a door and we were in the brightly lighted (bare bulbs on varying lengths of flex) cheerful-looking, bustling vestry where choir members were robing and collecting their music from a tumbling pile atop an impressive grand piano that took up a third of the entire floor space. Leaning against the piano a choirboy was listening vaguely to the Doc, a spare, very elegant elderly man who said to the boy, 'And comb your awful hair, and stop chewing! You are disgusting! And I thought I told you last Sunday to get your mother to wash your filthy surplice. You're a disgrace! Just see to it, boy!' The Doc turned and George introduced me. He had an instant, vigorous smile and a crushing hand grip. He watched the choirboy ambling away. 'Nice lad, that,' he said. 'Got the makings of a good voice. Turns up regularly and never gets sulky when I have to shout at him. I always have to shout at him. Wish we had more like him.'

The nice vicar materialized suddenly with his 'Good! Splendid! Great!' and introduced me to the new lady curate – she of the 'let's change everything' personality who was quite charming and asked me what kind of service I was used to. I told her and she smiled bravely. 'Yes,' she said, 'that's the kind of thing we do here, but …' and the charming smile *increased*, '…but we are going to do something about that. We have exciting plans, haven't we, vicar!' The nice vicar smiled and nodded and looked trapped and as they both moved away the Doc remarked reassuringly, 'We come across these types sometimes. They hold meetings and talk for hours. Then they

13

move on. I was a little worried about her ideas for the choir – but nothing to worry about . . . I think she's pretty harmless.'

I enjoyed the traditional Evensong service. There wasn't much room in the choir stalls, in fact they were overflowing because they had to accommodate a number of extra singers who had been invited for the special occasion – mostly former choir members who, over the years, had been thrown out of the choir for persistently wearing dirty white trainers in the choir stalls or showing a complete lack of musical ability. In his sermon the vicar said some nice things about the Doc and the choir and the crowded congregation clapped – much to the consternation of the vicar's warden who was not in favour of such a public demonstration, especially when it was in favour of the choir who already made enough noise anyway when they were singing and during the sermon when they were not singing.

George explained that the Doc had made it clear that he wanted no fuss at all over his birthday. He had directed that so long as the beautiful soprano sang 'Oh, for the wings of a dove' that strictly was to be all. Although, therefore, the evening was called the Doc's birthday 'do,' the coffee and chat feature that followed the service was very much the same as any other after-Evensong get-together. Nevertheless, nothing could stop the vicar climbing on a chair and repeating the part of his sermon in which he proclaimed that the Doc was Jolly Good! Splendid! Great! and asked what would we do without him and his wonderful choir? The vicar's warden was about to tell the people in his immediate vicinity just what they could do but at that moment a choir lady renowned for her gorgeous giant hot sausage rolls entered at the other end of the hall with a large tray of the monsters, preceded by her regal-looking tabby cat Robert who always sat under the pulpit during services and made a dignified exit right down the middle aisle if the vicar took more than his regulation ten minutes to deliver his sermon – which he often did.

There was a marked, indeed undignified, movement of guests towards the aroma of the hot sausage rolls and the new lady curate, who didn't like sausage rolls any more than Victorian hymns and didn't understand cats, was swept along on the hungry tide. She had planned to use the occasion to forward her ideas for transforming the church into a vibrant up-to-date community but perhaps this evening was not exactly the best time to start. But certainly she, with the carefully guided assistance of the nice vicar, would transform this church. George handed her a steaming sausage roll. Robert, who through long parish experience knew exactly how to deal with awkward characters, set himself at her feet purring loudly and turned his wondrous, magic tiger gaze on her – or on her sausage roll. The new lady curate felt strangely elated. It was going to be a job and a half converting this lot but it would be done. The church in this place would go forward. Her eyes were drawn irresistibly to the luminous green of Robert's unblinking gaze. And yes, he was absolutely right. In their new age, revitalized church no sermon would last longer than ten minutes!

3

We've Never Been Very Radical Here

It was a beautiful, warm, quiet Sunday afternoon in late summer in the picture-book-perfect village where my friend Arthur has the good fortune to live and write and to sing in the village church choir. We were sitting on a step of the handsome manor house tomb which gently dominated the churchyard and ivy-bound Georgian church. Arthur settled himself more comfortably against the white marble robe of the presiding angel who was pointing upwards, away from the earthly paradise of the village, and Arthur's big tabby cat, Thane, sprawled regardless, elegantly fast asleep on the sun-warmed memorial plaque recalling the worthy qualities of two centuries of local Lords of the Manor.

'Y'see,' said Arthur presently, 'the fact is that everything in the village is going fine – always has been as far as I know, especially at the church, so I reckon that people felt why change anything while we're so happy doing what we're doing? In my dad's young days we did have electric light put in the church but the new lamps in the stalls were all shaped like oil lamps – we've never been radical here. And that's quite something these days, isn't it! We get very good congregations here every Sunday and there's no feuds about changing the hymn book or sacking the organist, no yearning to rip out all the pews to make room for the kiddies' country dancing classes that are managing perfectly well in the village hall. There are no demands for plans to widen and surface the cart track that leads to the church so that parishioners can actually drive their cars right up to the church door without having to walk a single step!'

'A happy, hardy enthusiastic lot, you all sound,' I said.

'Exactly,' he agreed, 'and no one minds the racket kicked up by the kids at the back of the church right through the family service. Admittedly, sometimes you can't hear everything the vicar's saying in the sermon but you can always ask him about it over coffee and biscuits after the service, or if you really don't enjoy the kids creating havoc at the family service you can simply go to choral matins where everyone is quite proper, sitting in their favourite pews, smartly attired, the vicar doesn't have to shout the sermon and the congregation take it in turns to invite him to Sunday lunch.' Arthur paused and surveyed the peaceful scene comfortably. 'So, you see, everyone is catered for and no one rocks the boat. Of course, there is always the choir. Most of them have been around since before most of the rest of us were born – I'm their youngest member, so they go their own way and they could rock the boat but the vicar and the congregation put up with a good grace – a fine Christian spirit – the choir's, er, overwhelming musical input to the services, especially their "choir only" items which are all very loud – thunderous in fact – and go on and on and take up over half the service time. Still, some of the congregation reckons that the choir stuff is more inspiring than the vicar's sermon stuff anyway.' Arthur smiled reflectively. 'The choir are held in great respect, y'see. After all, where would we be in the church without someone who understands how to make the church boiler work during cold snaps, or where would we get enough labour to keep the churchyard in presentable condition and for replacing light bulbs up in the chancel ceiling while teetering on a convulsing ladder? And who could better our traditional Christmas carolling round the pubs that rakes in so much cash for our pensioners? Members of the choir do all that kind of thing as well as always bawling gentle, meditative hymns at the tops of their voices.'

'I should think the choir are very popular in the parish,' I said. 'A force for good indeed.'

'Oh, we are, we are,' Arthur readily agreed. 'The congregation really do appreciate all our efforts – except our singing efforts, of course.'

'I suppose it's all a matter of taste,' I suggested. 'Most church choirs are individualistic (or downright cussed) and sometimes find themselves at odds with the vicar and congregation.'

Arthur agreed again. 'Entirely jokingly of course,' he assured, 'our vicar calls our choir stick-in-the-mud, Victorian, lacking in any finer feelings – whatever they are – and undemocratic. And – entirely jokingly of course – the choir considers him a nice man but by far the most boring, unmusical vicar we've ever had to put up with. Everything is most civilized though. There are no squabbles on the church council and we all hang together in that sense of togetherness which the vicar is always on about.'

'That's an interesting way of looking at things,' I said.

'Well, it's the way we've carried on here for ages,' Arthur confirmed proudly. The first member of my family to join the choir was my great-grandfather who was here in the 1840s. He was the leading singer. He'd earned this position because he was generally two or three words ahead of the rest of the choir in the hymns. He believed in getting a move on, y'see. He never waited for the others to catch up. It was a mixed choir and the eight or nine young women they had were very good. Sometimes they sang so loudly that they put the men off key. They were a challenge to the men, y'see, and when the men took up the challenge the whole thing got faster and more and more exciting and caught up and passed the leading singer. There was a sturdy sense of purpose in the choir then. All members were present regularly every Sunday. Well – one or two tenors and basses were occasionally absent owing to their being in the village lock-up for poaching. Luckily the local magistrate liked the choir so there was no question of transportation and the poachers were out of the lock-up in no time.' Arthur grinned. 'I bet our vicar today would like to have our choir and organist shoved into the lock-up sometimes after we've sung "Abide with me" in the manner of the Soldiers' Chorus from "Faust".'

Chin in hands, Arthur gazed across at the snuggling little church. 'They didn't have an organ here in those days or choir stalls. The choir all sat up in the gallery on wooden forms with no backs with a bass fiddle player and a man with a trumpet who'd been in the cavalry at Waterloo. Only the choir ever went up in the gallery. The

19

congregation and the vicar never went near it. It had a reputation of being a mysterious, even evil, place, which for some reason housed two mantraps of gruesome reputation and the place was considered only fit for the resident gang of rats and the choir and great-grandad's cat, who kept the rats under control. He was a very big cat and had paws like a tiger's and was very unfriendly if he didn't know you or if you looked like the vicar. He had one green eye and one blue one.'

Arthur rose from our perch on the Manor House tomb, making a wide sweeping gesture over the ancient higgledy-piggledy grave stones and aged leaning angels. 'Great-grandad's choir are all around here,' he reflected, 'and their descendants have carried on the good work right down to the present day. Of course, we are down in the chancel now in posh choir stalls with the organ, but I reckon the descendants of the gallery rats are still around up there – under the supervision of Thane these days!'

'Perhaps Thane is a descendant of your great-grandad's cat,' I joked. On hearing his name mentioned the splendid tabby raised his head and opened his eyes wide. One eye was green and one was blue.

4

The Opener of the Windows

I reckon that my cousin Hector has opened more windows than any other man.

Wherever he goes, no matter what the weather, he opens windows. Buses and trains are his favourite haunts. As soon as he takes his seat he lowers the nearest window or, if it is already lowered, he lowers it still more, and if anyone starts to complain he immediately reels off a lecture about the danger to health from fuggy, germ-laden atmospheres.

It's just the same in friends' houses and public halls. He always manages to open about half-a-dozen windows, and it's useless to try to stop him because he thinks he is doing everyone a kindness. And my cousin Hector is a very kindly man.

Of course, he can't open windows when he visits cinemas, but he insists on sitting near an exit door, and he's caused no end of misunderstandings with usherettes who won't let him have a door ajar.

He loves fresh air. Many years ago, in the days of my youth, he took me up on Beachy Head in what appeared to be the most ferocious gale in history. He slapped me on the back – besides being kindly he is very hearty – and told me to square my shoulders, throw out my chest and take in great lungfuls of the fine, clean, health-giving air. It was also curiously strong air because it blew me over twice and each time I tried to take in a great lungful it took my breath away and nearly choked me to death.

Cousin Hector said he couldn't understand the molly-coddled young men of today. He said that in his day young men would have revelled in standing on Beachy Head and taking in great lungfuls of fine, clean, health-giving air.

And then, one Sunday during one of my infrequent visits to him, cousin Hector suddenly realized that there were some stained glass windows in his parish church which could actually be opened. The revelation came during the sermon at Matins. It was Midsummer Day, and the sky was suitably leaden and had been hurling down torrents of rain for hours and hours.

When we arrived at the church – a little late, owing to cousin Hector's insistence that I should wear a pair of his cast-off gumboots which were three sizes too large for me, and in which I could hardly move – we found the congregation standing in the mediaeval gloom and staring resentfully at their hymn books opened at 'Now that the daylight fills the sky'. They could have seen the words more clearly and glared more resentfully if the electric lights had been turned on. But apparently the chief sides-man was also the church treasurer and he was a very careful man, known in the secret places of the parish as Wary Wally. His reasoning seemed to be that as Matins was scheduled to take place during daylight hours there could never be any need for artificial lights. So when Wary Wally prowled the aisles they never had lights at Matins.

When the service reached the point for the sermon, the congregation was even less ready this morning than usual to lend an ear to what the vicar was mumbling about. They just sat there as some congregations do sit, letting their eyes and thoughts wander all over the church and as far away from the pulpit as possible.

Then it was that cousin Hector spotted, with a tremendous thrill, an ancient remnant of cord hanging rather dejectedly from the top of the stained glass window nearest him. Further exciting scrutiny – this involved cousin Hector swivelling right round and thoroughly embarrassing a very small lady with a very big hat immediately behind us, by squinting fanatically over her head – revealed that every other window in the church was made to open at the top. The full-length figures depicted in them were mostly of saints and past local aldermen, and the movable hinged sections at the top contained their heads. To open the windows, the idea, presumably, was to persuade the saints and past local aldermen to bow their heads when necessary. You did this by tugging on a long cord which was attached to the top of the window and reached you down the wall via a fantastically clever contraption of wheels, springs and bent nails which seldom worked, at the first or second attempt.

At the close of the service, cousin Hector told me to wait for a minute, and lurked about behind a pillar until the vicar had finished shaking hands with everybody and enquiring after the health of their babies, their lodgers and their dear old grandparents, who were all sitting at home doing nothing and waiting for their Sunday lunch.

Then cousin Hector pounced, and pronounced simply and finally, 'We must have these windows open, vicar. They can't have been opened for years. An absolute danger to health. I'll fix them up with new cords tomorrow evening.'

The vicar, a small and elderly bachelor, lived in constant terror of draughts, and had jammed up most of the fine old gaping Regency windows of the vicarage with wads of parish magazines. He also lived in constant terror of cousin Hector. Cousin Hector had a very loud voice, and if he didn't get what he wanted on the church council it became louder and louder.

'Yes – yes . . .' enthused the vicar, backing away hurriedly. 'Open the windows – yes – well, of course. Good, good . . .' and he faded into the vestry, hoping devoutly that cousin Hector wouldn't terrify him any more that day. What with the ceiling leaking all over the front pew at the early service and ruining the hideous new dress of that enormous woman from Elfin Cottage, and the choir on the verge of rebellion because he gave the tiniest hint that he was thinking of changing the hymn book, and the bishop announcing that he was going to 'drop in' next week, 'just to see how the happy family are', the vicar thought that he'd just about had enough without some fool opening all the windows.

He bundled himself into the well-loved raincoat with one button and a leather belt, which he wore at all times and in all places, and let himself out into the churchyard into a particularly jolly surge of wind and rain and dead flowers from an overturned dustbin. He squelched slowly down the path to the vicarage, dutifully endeavouring to keep in place a happy Christian smile, in case he met anyone who was in a worse mess that he was and needed a bit of encouragement.

He tried to think of a peaceful, serene world full of golden light, where ceilings didn't leak all over terrible females, and there were no windows to open, and the only choirs were those like they had in films, where they made beautiful sounds behind sunsets and were never seen.

Meanwhile, as I stumbled from the church in cousin Hector's gigantic cast-off rubber boots, he boomed away gaily about what we were going to do on the morrow. He said that we were very lucky really, because it happened that a builder who had been messing about in the church had left a long ladder lying down the side aisle and that was the very thing we could do with. He said that he'd let me go up the ladder, and he would stand at the bottom and tell me what to do. He reckoned that the windows hadn't been opened for about 50 years, and it would be a really interesting challenge to me. He said it was the kind of interesting challenge that the young men of his day would have revelled in . . .

Early the next evening, cousin Hector fitted me out with a boiler suit my size, covered with a fascinating mixture of paint and coke dust, and in no time at all I was up the ladder working away feverishly with a hammer and screwdriver under his reassuringly bawled directions. I worked conscientiously and exactly as ordered, and after half an hour I'd made no impression whatsoever on the rusted-in head of the past local alderman who kept on glaring at me in a most disconcerting manner. I was beginning seriously to think of myself as an utter failure, when I heard the vicar's voice far below. I could never hear a word he said in his sermons, but now I heard the word 'tea' – 'tea' very clearly . . .

We sat comfortably in the unbelievable chaos of the vicar's study. Somehow, in his study, he was a different man.

'And talking of windows,' he was saying, as he poured cousin Hector a fourth cup of overpoweringly strong tea. 'I'm almost afraid to mention it' – and he didn't seem the slightest bit afraid – 'but I've been having a little trouble with the window of my new shed. It's supposed to open, but I can't budge it. I wondered if, before you go back to the church, you would – er – have a look at it?'

No appeal to open a window could possibly fail to move cousin Hector. Suddenly he was down at the bottom of the vicarage garden.

'Leave this to me!' we heard him bawl joyously. 'I know how to deal with this kind!'

Some three hours later, when the natural dusk of the English summer day was being rapidly deepened by some natural solid black clouds of the English summer day, the vicar and I stood watching cousin Hector from the study window.

'A happy man,' murmured the vicar. 'A happy man.'

He was still working on the shed. By this time he appeared to have half demolished it, and the offending window had been shifted. In fact, it lay all over the lawn in a hundred splinters. The vicar must have sensed that somehow I was still not really as thrilled as I should have been at the prospect of returning up the ladder to face the interesting challenge of the unresponsive past local alderman's head. He beamed at me his happy Christian smile, reserved for those who were in a bigger mess than he was.

'I'm afraid – I'm very much afraid – that you will have to forget about the church windows this time,' he apologized. 'I am certainly most grateful to you, most grateful, but by the time your – er – cousin has finished with my shed, it will be too late to go back to the church – there'll be a choir practice going on anyway and we don't want to upset that lot – and then early tomorrow the builder is coming for his ladder.'

I think the vicar liked me. Perhaps he recognized a fellow sufferer. He poured me a cup of tea from a newly made pot, and his happy Christian smile widened into something suspiciously near a roguish grin.

5

A Nice Quiet Interlude

Somewhere in the wilds of Suffolk my friend Timmy is a member of a village church choir that consists mainly of an old-established, much revered 'back row of the chorus' group. These characters are devoted to the choir but they don't actually sing very much, indeed two of them merely mime. Traditionally, they leave the real singing to three or four members, including Timmy, who can read music and sing all the solos and generally make enough noise to smother any odd sounds coming from the back row members who always sing very softly anyway so that the organist can't identify anyone who is singing flat or coming in at the wrong place.

Timmy is, in fact, acting organist, an honorary title he earned after the previous organist, having served in the post for 20 years, moved to London on his eightieth birthday in search of a more active, exciting musical career. That was ten years ago and the old organist has achieved his aim, becoming the senior conductor of a famous brewery brass band. Meanwhile Timmy is still serving as acting organist at his village church. The parochial church council have fully intended to advertise for a new official organist over the past ten years – they often mention the matter at regular meetings but have not quite got round to doing anything about it yet.

Now Timmy was on the phone to me with an urgent request. On Sunday, the vicar – with half the congregation – would be away on a retreat and a friend of the vicar's, a recently ordained young woman who was temporarily working in the parish, would be standing in for him at the Sunday morning service.

'Ordained young woman!' I repeated. 'That's something new for your parish, isn't it?'

'True,' he admitted. 'We haven't had one of those before. Bridget is something out of the ordinary too. She looks sort of ethereal, smiles at everyone all the time. She's got a lovely, kindly smile – not gushing like the vicar's wife when she's trying to recruit people to do a stint on church cleaning Saturday. It's a sort of faraway smile and looking like she's thinking beautiful, serene thoughts – ethereal, she's that type.'

'Quite a change from your vicar,' I reckoned.

'Oh, yes,' he agreed. 'You couldn't really call him ethereal. He's down to earth, y'see – keeps on shaking hands with well-off people at meetings and saying the church urgently needs lots more money so that he can have the Victorian pews ripped out and a kiddies' cycle track laid round the churchyard.' Timmy growled something I didn't quite catch and then continued, 'anyway to return to our latest dilemma, on Sunday, quite coincidentally, the choir will also be much depleted – not that any of us will be on the retreat, you understand – our choir never retreats, but all our main singers will be away. Our bass soloist, he of the outraged football hooligan voice, will be

29

at the Rose and Crown darts tournament final, our two tenors – the one who follows the music very precisely and the one who follows his own inclinations very loudly – are on holiday, and our sensational young soprano soloist who is excellent at raising the roof in a magnificent Wagnerian manner even when she's supposed to be performing gentle, meditative passages, is going to an important Sunday dog show with her champion Rottweiler. He's gorgeous! He comes to church sometimes and keeps the noisy kids in order.'

'So you are left with just the back row whisperers – and your good self,' I added encouragingly.

'Unfortunately, not even my good self,' confessed Timmy. 'The soaking we all got last Saturday when I was leading our "mystery parish walk" in aid of the junior church's summer outing has bestowed on me the grandfather of all sore throats – can't you tell? I shall be joining the back row whisperers on Sunday.' He groaned noisily down the phone, 'and that's not all! The organ blowing motor has burned out – it's been burning out for years and the church council have been going to do something about it for years, so it's not really surprising – just awkward because it would happen for this particular Sunday and I've got to rely on the vestry piano which saw its best days half a century ago before being pensioned off from a Thames pleasure steamer.' He groaned again even more loudly. 'So what do you say? Can you help us out on Sunday? After all, you do sing a bit louder than our back row of the chorus and most of the time anyway you are more or less in tune. It would encourage some of us to have a more determined go at the hymns.'

When one is offered such a flattering invitation how can one do other than accept? . . .

From the nearest railway station a nearly empty, very reluctant bus – it kept on slowing down between stops and stopping for minutes at stops where no one was waiting – eventually brought me to the end of its meanderings opposite the lych-gate of Timmy's village church. The church, a long low ivy-clad building with a fat little tower that seemed to consist mainly of three huge, sprawling clock faces and some demonic gargoyles, crouched behind a row of austere poplars who looked as though they were trying to ignore the rustic jumble behind them. I now realized that, despite the efforts of the languid bus, I was more than a little early for the morning service. The church door was locked – and the only living occupants of the church-yard apart from me were a familiar big ex-rugger type with a large very attractive-looking puppy. Timmy loped towards me and grasped my hand in a paralysing grip. He beamed at me and I beamed at the outsize puppy.

'How about him!' Timmy enthused. 'I'm just giving him a run before church. He's gorgeous, don't you think?' The puppy rolled on his back energetically and Timmy seemed to detect that I was wondering which breed he was. 'He's a sort of Bulldog,' he explained. 'Sort of, because we don't actually know who his father was.' All three of us wandered around the churchyard while Timmy explained that he was endeavouring to teach his sort of Bulldog puppy to behave respectfully at services and that the choir stalls were out of bounds for him, they being the abode of the Wagnerian soprano soloist's Rottweiler, Karl, who would stand no nonsense.

He said he didn't have to worry about the other animal who attended the services, the vicar's cat Bert, because, in the manner of cats, Bert ran the whole show anyway and no one argued with him. He always sat under the pulpit during the service and if the vicar exceeded ten minutes for his mini-sermon, walked out very regally, right down the middle aisle, completely breaking the spell of the vicar's oratory. Timmy said the congregation and the choir were regularly very grateful to Bert on Sunday mornings.

'So what do you think will happen at this morning's service,' I asked, 'with the vicar away and this new lady priest preaching? What about Bert's ten-minute limit on sermons?' Timmy waved a hand dismissively. 'Oh the lady will be all right there. The couple of times she has preached she's finished well inside the ten minutes allowance. Y'see, she agrees with Bert that sermons should be fleeting, she likes to mix with the congregation and chat informally and quietly about things that matter – not talk at them from the pulpit with a mic. Most of the congregation seem to like this innovation although one or two who normally nod off now and then do find the situation a bit trying.'

While we walked and talked in the churchyard someone had unlocked the church and in the choir vestry we came across a handful of the back row of the chorus choir members who were sorting their cassocks and surplices from a pile draped across the veteran piano. Timmy introduced me to one or two members who hadn't been around during my last visit two years ago and told them that I'd come from London to help them out, and an ancient bass gentleman butted in and said yes he remembered me doing that the last time I was there when the choir broke down in the middle of the Te Deum and I didn't know the anthem. Timmy's sort of Bulldog puppy disentangled a wreck of a cassock from the pile on the piano – obviously a favourite of his – and started dragging it around the vestry floor in a frenzy of delight. Timmy quickly rescued it and, holding its tatters aloft, said yes, this was the one I had last time – it was a perfect fit. He helped me on with it and announced that we'd all better look at the hymns for the service to make sure everyone knew them and wouldn't be wary about singing out without the support of the absent principals. Everyone reckoned that we could just about do this as long as there was big support from the piano. Timmy suggested that we would sing one verse of Bach's 'Jesu, Joy' for the anthem and this was readily agreed because the choir had sung it at almost every wedding, christening and funeral service for the last 40 years. Timmy said people around the parish didn't go in much for change and so you always knew where you were with the music. I asked Timmy who actually chose the music for the services, was it the organist or the vicar? There were countless stories of feuds between the two throughout the Church of England. 'The organist,' Timmy announced firmly. 'You really can't have unmusical types like clergy messing about with the music.'

'That should be left to the experts,' I said.

'Absolutely,' he agreed. 'Mind you, we've had some pretty ruthless types here as organist. I've sometimes felt for the vicar. Take our last official organist, a real character. Absolute dictator, autocratic slave driver, a perfect example of mannerless arrogance. But, so what? He could have been a lot worse – what about the man we had before him who used to slurp onion soup and crunch crisps at the organ right through the sermon at Matins. Yes, he did take a lot of putting up with, but there again, he never called the choir a bunch of mindless musical morons like the man before him did. You have to take the rough with the smooth.'

We didn't get any further with Timmy's history of the village organists as the new stand-in lady priest now gently materialized, a graceful young figure in an immaculate cassock that swirled around her so that she appeared to float before us and envelop us in the glorious smile that had so captivated Timmy. The ancient bass growled to me that she only looked like that because her cassock was two sizes too big for her and she had to swirl it about a bit so as not to tread on it and trip up . . .

The service went well. The congregation, perhaps realizing the reduced state of the choir, loyally sang the hymns instead of merely opening their hymn books and gazing about the church. And just now and again you might have detected a shy note or two from the back row of the chorus, where I wasn't helping much, having somehow got hold of the wrong hymn book.

In the choir vestry after the service the stand-in lady priest's famous ethereal smile magnified. 'Thank you, choir,' she beamed. 'It was so good to hear the hymns sung so gently, quietly, thoughtfully. You created that wonderful, prayerful atmosphere – a simple beautiful experience so far removed from the, er, football match rowdy insensitive . . . er . . . shouting one hears so much in churches these days. I so look forward to hearing you all again at Evensong tonight.' The ancient bass responded eagerly. 'It'll be even better tonight,' he claimed. 'All the solo people will be back in time for the service. They'll get going with "Battle Hymn of the Republic". It's our specialty, we do it with a descant. We'll raise the roof! You'll love it.'

The lady's ethereal smile was still there – although, as Timmy noted as we waited at the station for my train, there was something sort of different about it, a sort of *frozen* ethereal smile.

6

The Suspended Career

Teddy is one of my oldest church friends. We joined the
church choir on the same day when we were nine years
old – and Teddy was ejected from that choir as musically
useless just three weeks later. His parents were sorry but
not surprised at the choirmaster's decision. In prepara-
tion for his career as a chorister Teddy's father had tried
to get him to sing a well-known hymn somewhat rec-
ognizably in tune in a more-or-less human voice to the
accompaniment, variously, of a trombone, a harp, a flute
and finally, in desperation, a mouth organ. When his
mother took him to his first choir practice she told the
choirmaster that he had had a bad cold and sore throat
but he would soon be in full voice again and really showing what he could do.

This Teddy duly did with shattering effect that ended
his very brief choir career on the spot. He still liked going to church, however, and became an altar server and,
in after years, much involved with the parochial church
council and with subduing and seeking to enlighten the
more violent elements in the Sunday School. Seemingly
tireless, he had also organized campaigns for reclaiming
the churchyard from totally wild nature and rescuing the
longsuffering church organ from finally falling to bits.

Recently, Teddy, who is a genuine confirmed bachelor (with his notorious tabby tom cat who certainly isn't), retired from his City job to a place in the country, a distinctly pretty village which still has a post office, a live pub and a busy church with a real vicar and the biggest ramshackle choir for miles for whom 'loud' and 'very loud' are always lovely and inspiring, supported by an organist whose devoted Wagnerian leanings lead the singers in thunderous praise throughout every service.

And to that church recently came my friend Teddy and when, as a member of the congregation, he had partaken in his first service there in which the triumphant roar of choir and organ has swept away all negative thoughts and impressions, he suddenly knew that after these many, many years, here was his unique opportunity, here was a choir and organist who would surely not reject him on the grounds that he couldn't sing and would enable him thrillingly to re-start his early interrupted singing career with a vengeance!

At the close of the service Teddy made for the choir vestry and eagerly pushed his way in against a tide of choir people eagerly pushing their way out in the direction of the next door tavern, a thatched-roof, shambling establishment called The Cracked Bell, named in honour of the tenor bell in the church tower that had been cracked since it was hung there in 1780 and urgently discussed by the church council ever since.

A choirboy, recognizing an enquiring stranger in the camp, informed Teddy, 'He's the one you want – the one over there with the red face. That's him, telling off our head choirboy. He always tells him off after the service because he says he can't hear him singing – well, who can hear him when he's stuck right next to the organ and in front of Ma Smith the alto lady? She's our head-mistress at the school and takes assembly every morning. Talk about shout! She sings like that too! Anyway, there's him wot plays the organ, over there with the red face. His face is not always red. It only gets like that when he's shouting at our head boy.' The head boy, dismissed by the organist with a final demand to 'make yourself heard at Evensong, for heaven's sake!', whisked around Teddy on a single skate and out of the vestry chuckling, 'Can't hear me! Rubbish, Tripe! He's getting past his sell-by date, that's what he's doing!'

The organist was pleased to meet Teddy and immediately welcomed him into the choir without even enquiring whether he sang alto, tenor or bass or anything in between. Teddy had described him to me as 'a dapper, middle-aged gent wearing an immaculate grey suit and red silk tie and gleaming expensive shoes who, in earlier times, would certainly have sported spats and probably a monocle'. Not without a note of pride, he told Teddy that the choir were very popular and indispensable on all kinds of festive occasions in the area. 'People still get married in these parts,' he explained, 'all church dos too! So we're busy on most spring and summer Saturdays. The vicar makes sure that wedding couples avoid the Saturdays when the darts team are playing away as most of the choir are in the team. And you really need the choir at church weddings because even if people sing in church on Sundays they're far too busy gawping at the bride and bridesmaids and the fancy hats, and videoing everything that moves, to spare time to sing hymns. Our vicar really appreciates the choir at these times. He's got a sort of nondescript singing voice – indescribable actually – that's full of enthusiasm, if you know what I mean, and he feels free to let himself go in the hymns at weddings because most of our tenors and basses sing like he does so his voice doesn't stand out awkwardly if he's too flat or sharp or uncontrollably ebullient.'

Over the weeks following Teddy's move to the country and subsequent entry into the village choir, I couldn't help wondering if history would repeat itself and he would be removed from the choir once they'd actually heard him 'joining in' with his unique versions of the music everyone else was more or less performing as the composer had planned.

I need not have worried. 'It really is an eye opener, singing in this choir,' Teddy enthused over the phone. 'Everyone sings so, er, sort of purposefully, powerfully, that it's easy for me to follow the most dominant voice and we all blend very well – well, all except the vicar. He's very individualistic in all things, you see, particularly in his vocal efforts, but he also likes to feel that he's very democratic and always lets the organist choose the hymns for the services and never disagrees with his choices even if the sentiments of the hymns are violently at odds with those that he is to champion in his sermon. The vicar is a downright believer in the modern church as a boundless fellowship of believers that encompasses all shades of opinion in one dedicated, united whole . . .'

After a few months during which his membership of the choir had already been overwhelmingly confirmed –

Teddy is an exceptionally good darts player and a wonderful asset to the choir team – he invited me to 'come down here and make a guest appearance in the choir stalls at a very special service'. The organist had apparently declared that any friend of Teddy's would be a friend of his and the choir's as long as he or she could be heard right down at the back row of the congregation where they never sang above a whisper even when they knew the hymns. All they seemed to do down there, the organist told Teddy, was to stop people sitting in other people's pews and making sure the sidesmen were there to take up the collection . . .

The special service turned out to be a celebration of the 90th birthday of a local character who had been a bell ringer at the church since being thrown out of the youth club at the age of 12 as wholly unmanageable and placed in the iron control of the bell captain who vowed that if he couldn't transform the little fiend in six months and turn him into a first-rate ringer, he'd resign. And he never resigned.

After the celebration service we all hurried off to the reception at the village hall where the veteran ringer was seated in an armchair closely surrounded by his wife and beaming colleagues all holding glasses of champagne and being nudged by smiling ladies balancing plates of miniature pork pies and little things on sticks. As the crowd swirled ever increasingly around the dispensers of alcoholic good cheer, and guests were finding it harder tracing continuing supplies of the very popular little things on sticks, I momentarily lost sight of Teddy and found myself hemmed into a corner with a large iron umbrella stand and three tightly packed elderly ladies from the choir who were apparently anxious to know what kind of singing voice mine was because it had been quite new to them during the service and in fact they'd never heard anything quite like it. Expressing surprised pleasure in their keen interest, I said I supposed I was a sort of alto or counter tenor and they nodded and said 'very interesting' and 'most unusual' and 'Ah! That explains it' and started talking amongst themselves excitedly, allowing me to escape and join Teddy who had suddenly reappeared firmly collared by the local newspaper reporter. She was an attractive, very young woman who was just reacting with breathless amazement at Teddy's revelation that he had first joined his church choir at the age of nine in a year which, to the youthful reporter, was obviously long lost, far, far back in the mists of ancient history. She gazed at him in awe. As I joined them Teddy informed her eagerly 'It's true! This man was there at the time!' She transferred her gaze to me and appeared even more awe-stricken, scribbled furiously in her notebook and moved on as the organist, immaculately attired as always, beamingly caught her eye . . .

A few days after I'd returned home I received from Teddy a sizeable cutting from his local paper. The headline was surprisingly big and black. 'OVER 75 YEARS A CHORISTER. Proud record of new member of St John's choir'. There followed a fulsome, enthusiastic account by the paper's new young journalist describing how Teddy had commenced his long singing career at the age of nine in his local church choir in the thirties of the last century and now, in the twenty-first century, had brought all his years of experience and expertise into the services of St John's choir in the village 'where he was delighted to retire – but not from singing!'

Sometimes there is a story which offers no foreseeable conclusion!

7

Saved by the Belle

'Our village church choir have always been there,' said my friend Sam proudly. 'They were there even before the church was built in 1880 to replace a corrugated iron mission hall that got so hot inside during the summer that they had to hold the services outside in a field with half-a-dozen Shire horses.'

'What about the organ?' I asked.

'Well, of course, they didn't have one of those in the tin church,' explained Sam. 'They had a sort of harmonium on some old pram wheels and they were able to push it into the field with the choir or around the village when they sang carols outside the big houses and inside the pubs at Christmas.'

'You've got a very big organ in the church now,' I said.

'Yes, it takes up half the left-hand aisle,' he agreed. 'It was given by a man who always did things in a big way. He owned the local brewery and never came to church on Sunday or any other time if he could help it. It was reckoned the organ was his sort of peace offering to the vicar and to ensure that the church would put on a good show for him when he was obliged to attend for family baptisms, weddings and funerals. He was a very generous man indeed and paid for electricity to be installed in the church even before they had it in the manor house or the railway station – well, they've only just got it at the railway station and it keeps on failing . . .'

When he died they buried him next to the lych-gate in an outsized tomb covered with marble angels and weeping women that remains prominent even at night in the light of a village street gas lamp that still defies the invasion of the brewer's new-fangled electricity.

'And the organ and choir are still flourishing today,' I said.

'Indeed,' enthused Sam. 'We've got a bigger choir than we've had for years and the organ is used more than ever, by Waistcoat' (the flamboyant bachelor organist and choirmaster, so called for his predilection for sporting highly coloured fancy velvet waistcoats, a different one for each day). Sam smiled resignedly. 'Of course, our new vicar, being a forward thinking cleric, is doing his best to get rid of the choir stalls, which he says are very old-fashioned and taking up the space in front of the altar that could be used for flower arrangements or, much more important, provide a central stage from which to deliver his "vital sermons" for which space is essential for his freedom of movement and dramatic poses and gestures and any "supporting cast" he may need to confirm his words – all of which would not be possible in the narrow confines of the pulpit which, he says, isolates him from the fellowship of the congregation.'

'What about the choir?' I asked.

'Oh, there's rumours that he wants to push them out of the way up in the gallery,' he said. 'The vicar's not a very musical person – well, not musical at all really – and says that too much singing restricts open discussion time during the service – that's when he puts forward his vital plans for bringing the church right into the twenty-first century and challenges the reactionaries in the congregation to stand up in their pews, behind their personal pillars, and be counted.'

Things could have gone badly for Waistcoat's choir but help was at hand. Hailed enthusiastically by the vicar, a newly ordained lady curate named Flavia joined the church staff. She was young, single, attractive (indeed the belle of the ball in Waistcoat's eyes) and go-ahead and full of admiration for the vicar's fearless crusading spirit. Her appointment was an essential part of the vicar's forward thinking. She was confident, would charm the stick-in-the-muds in the congregation to go forward boldly, to experiment, to embrace lively new ideas for worship and, most urgently, deal with the vexed question of the intrusive choir stalls and equally intrusive choirs who were firmly stuck in the nineteenth century with the organist's waistcoats – and hadn't the faintest intention of going forward anywhere from their choir stalls. Unfortunately, however, Flavia possessed, and liked to use, an outstanding soprano singing voice, a fact that she had modestly omitted to mention to the vicar during her interviews for the post.

Unaware of the new curate's musical talents, Waistcoat and the choir were therefore somewhat surprised when, during her first week in the parish, she appeared beaming excitedly during the Friday evening choir practice while the choir were at full blast halfway through one of their favourite, gloriously florid Victorian settings of the Te Deum. She seated herself elegantly at the empty end of a choir stall, closed her eyes and appeared as one enchanted. Now, as Sam said when recounting the latest parish news to me, no one in the choir thought of themselves or their voices as being actually enchanting – they were a reasonably acceptable crowd with a pretty passable organist and choirmaster, but hardly an enchanting choir – not unless you compare them with the parish church choir. Then, of course, they appear most enchanting as do any other band of singers when compared with the parish church choir. The parish church choir are the biggest choir for miles around. They overflow the choir stalls, seldom have any practices, and regularly dominate the football crowd singing uproar at every local match. It was generally accepted by musically inclined churchgoers that whereas Waistcoat's choir were not at all bad, although unfortunately purely Victorian, the parish church choir were unfortunately purely brute force and ignorance.

When the choir had finished singing the Te Deum, Waistcoat expressed his and the choir's very great pleasure at having the new lady curate with them and invited her to join them for the rest of the practice. She said she'd be absolutely delighted to, and long before the end of the practice they all realized that here they had a soloist par excellence.

Waistcoat was never one to miss an opportunity and here he saw a huge one. Immediately after the practice finished he confronted the new lady curate with his well-known choirmasterful pose. Thumbs stuck in the top of his puce and lemon shaded velvet waistcoat he regarded her with his most overwhelmingly attractive smile. 'Verily, you are a godsend,' he purred, 'a veritable godsend! Y'see, since our solo boy's voice broke a few months ago there has been no one else ready to take over the solo part in "Hear My Prayer" – you know – the "O for the wings of a dove" bit – our traditional showpiece for all big occasions. We had almost given up hope of doing it next time – the vicar's birthday this coming Sunday, as it happens.' He unhooked his thumbs from his waistcoat and raised his hands as if in blessing. His smile became even more overwhelming, 'and now you are here!'

The vicar's belated discovery that the new lady curate was a talented soprano who not only loved singing at every opportunity, but especially singing sentimental Victorian anthems with Waistcoat's intrusively hide-bound choir, was a jarring obstacle to his programme of arranging for her future in the forward-thinking twenty-first century church. For his previous birthday celebration service, when he'd only just arrived in the parish, he had had to sit through the choir's rendering of 'Hear My Prayer', anxiously counting the seconds to when he could come amongst the congregation and start up another 'free and open discussion' to ensure that everyone eagerly, democratically welcomed and agreed with his firm plans for the thrilling future of their church – plans that definitely didn't include the choir stalls and the choir cluttering up the chancel and spoiling everything.

And now, another birthday Evensong was upon him and still the awful choir stalls and choir were there, getting in the way of progress, intruding unfeelingly into his cherished mental picture of the chancel filled with exotic flowers and with the preacher centre stage inspiring the whole congregation to immerse themselves in vital meaningful discussion with wine and nibbles at the back of the church after the service. As the clergy and choir shuffled themselves in procession to enter the church for the vicar's latest birthday Evensong, he approached the next hour with positive joyful expectation in his heart together with just a mite of anxiety. This was the occasion when he had decided to put forward with firmness (gentle firmness, of course) his master plan to eliminate the choir stalls and transform the chancel into a place of peace and beauty and inspiration. He realized that this evening he'd have to put up with 'Hear My Prayer' once again, the choir's traditional birthday tribute to the last three vicars (the choir were so very traditional), but hopefully this *would* be the final time and then they would be out of sight in the gallery or, much better still, gone off to join the riotous ranks of the parish church choir. They would enjoy themselves there – and the vicar liked to know people were enjoying themselves. It was a pity that the lady curate had turned out to be a solo singer, he hoped she wouldn't sing too many solos – she would *encourage* the choir. And that was the last thing the vicar wanted. Nevertheless, things, he felt, were progressing well and it was his birthday and his loyal parishioners were here in force for him (or for the beer, as one or two tasteless choir men had suggested).

The vicar beamed at the packed congregation and announced the first hymn, 'Through all the changing scenes of life'. He smiled into his little-used hymn book.

Yes, he liked that title. There was going to be a changing scene right here in his church and the congregation would surely be happy about it – even inspired, once the scene minus the awful Victorian choir stalls and choir became a reality. Enthusiastically, quite unexpected, and to the consternation of the choir man nearest to him, the vicar joined in the singing vigorously, noisily and well ahead of the organ. The choir man was indeed shocked. Previously he'd never noticed the vicar even opening his hymn book with any alacrity of purpose beyond eventually glancing at the right page and looking away immediately to gaze disapprovingly at the Victorian stained glass window above the altar. The choir man was now most concerned – shocked. What on earth was the vicar up to now – actually bawling out a Victorian hymn and looking *pleased*?

I was not present at the vital service but friend Sam gave me a blow-by-blow report on its startling climax. 'When the anthem was announced, the congregation, as usual, settled themselves comfortably into their pews for their little break and the singing began. Of course, as the choir had "done this one" for umpteen special services no one was afraid of singing out and making the same mistakes that we'd made for years but it sounded all right to us and we were pretty well together and in tune as we came to the part when the soloist starts off – the "O for the wings of a dove" bit.' Sam paused with a look of wonder on his face. 'Well, you wouldn't believe this if you hadn't been there. Flavia had only sung a few bars when the whole atmosphere seemed to spring to life, even in the back rows of the congregation where normally there's no animation at all. You could see them suddenly stirring and taking notice.' Sam's eyes widened. 'It was wonderful. I reckon none of us had ever heard a voice like that in our church. It was thrilling – sort of riveting, and when the choir came in again in the chorus parts we sounded absolutely terrific. We were all looking amazed – it was magic. Waistcoat had never got us to sing like that. Talk about a miracle! Then something happened that I've never even dreamed could happen in our church. As the anthem finished, the whole congregation – even the back rows – burst into applause, clapping madly, stamping their feet and there were "bravos" coming from all over the place.' Sam was beaming with the thought of it all. 'And what about this! Everyone went on clapping for so long that Waistcoat signalled that we sing the anthem again. And we did. I couldn't see the vicar's face but he was sitting there very still.'

The merry disturbance quietened at last and the vicar stood up. He had his 'get rid of the choir stalls' sermon notes with him but he quickly put them out of sight in his cassock pocket. 'And how can I follow that?' he asked. 'It is truly wonderful that you all have taken to heart so enthusiastically Flavia, the newest member of our team. With her glorious voice she is indeed welcome in our choir – our choir,' he heard himself saying, 'who unfailingly, Sunday by Sunday, are up there in the chancel leading us in songs of praise – uniting us! I look forward to a period of great spiritual revival and flowering of community spirit in the parish.'

Sam smiled an enigmatic smile. 'Give the vicar his due, you know. He's not narrow-minded. He's always ready to see another way – especially when he realizes he's not going to get his way.' Still with a lingering tone of amazement, he recounted then how, at the wine and nibbles gathering at the back of the church after the service, enthusiastic parishioners surrounded Flavia the new curate and super-soloist, overwhelming her with a flood of extravagant praise and even acknowledging some other members of the choir with almost warm smiles. Normally, nobody smiled much at the choir. They were just a handful of outlandish characters who appeared every Sunday up there in the choir stalls and disappeared rapidly after the service (mostly to the George and Dragon) through a discreet back door, thus mostly avoiding the huge congestion in the church porch where everyone was shaking hands with the vicar and congratulating him on his sermon or saying how much they liked the new fluorescent church notice board outside the lych-gate.

My friend ended his story with an exaggerated sigh. 'So it looks as though our future in the choir stalls is safe enough for a while now – and the parish church choir will have to do without us after all,' he grinned.

'They'll manage,' I said, 'as long as there are football matches, they'll manage!'

8

Do You Qualify?

In my experience daughter churches are often superior to parish churches. Invariably they attract the best preachers. They also attract the people who consider themselves the best choristers.

The choirs of daughter churches get invited to sing at cathedrals, and are always winning cups at music festivals, but among parish church choirs you will find many a cheerful shambles. They never get invited to sing anywhere, are incapable of winning anything, and can sing much louder than three or four daughter church choirs put together.

When I told a relative with whom I was staying in rural Somerset that I should like to sing Evensong in the choir of a certain nearby church he warned me off immediately. 'Don't go there,' he advised. 'You wouldn't get into *that* choir anyway. You go down to the parish church. They're far easier there and more up your street.'

I thanked him for being so helpful, but was naturally curious to learn more about the unapproachable church. Apparently it was a very exclusive place and ranked socially with the local golf club. In fact, it was an unwritten law that you should be a member of the golf club before you joined the church.

From time to time some rude, pushing person tried to gate-crash without the backing of the club, but they were always expertly put in their place. They were warmly welcomed and someone would immediately fix them up with the job of stoking the church boiler, cleaning the inaccessible clerestory windows or polishing about half a ton of brass ornaments. This got rid of them in no time at all, and they soon found their proper level at the parish church. This was a venerable ruin full of the most awful people who couldn't tell one end of a golf club from the other and boasting the largest, most unmanageable apology for a choir for miles.

After a few moments' searching questioning, the vicar directed me unerringly to the parish church. I went directly to the choir vestry, knowing from experience that if you enter by the main door and try to explain to the churchwarden that you want to join the choir, he either looks at you as if you are mad or pushes some books into your hand and says you can sit anywhere.

I also knew from experience that the choir vestry door is always the one round the back, often half hidden behind a mountain of coke and dustbins full of dead flowers. So I entered the place with perfect confidence, and was soon happily in the middle of a dozen members of the choir who were all trying to robe within ten square feet.

The organist declared that he was delighted to see me, particularly as I was an alto, because five of the gentlemen present were basses and things sometimes got a bit top-heavy . . . In the chancel there were three rows of choir stalls on either side, and the curate waited politely while we all arranged ourselves in each other's elbow-room. When we eventually attacked the first hymn I didn't seem to have a hymn book, but a number of others didn't either. There was in consequence much shuffling of books and I almost got one by the end of the third verse. Someone did in fact toss me one but someone else immediately grabbed it away again. By the time we reached the last verse I had settled down to share a book with my neighbour. He was a very short gentleman who appeared to be suffering from a frightful cold – or perhaps he normally sang like that. Anyway the book was half obliterated by a large red handkerchief which trailed from inside his sleeve and allowed me to see only the hymn we weren't singing on the opposite page.

No one sat below me, so later in the service I edged to the end of the stall in order to examine a pile of rubbish which I thought might contain a hymn book. It was then that I noticed on the floor what appeared to be a moth-eaten hearth rug. When, however, it began to wag its tail furiously I realized that it was some sort of dog. He was a most friendly freak and, I learned later, was the bosom pal of the bachelor curate. Unlike so many clergymen, the curate apparently didn't think it sinful and didn't verge on apoplexy every time an animal looked inside a church. The hearth rug certainly didn't look very sinful. He was most intelligent too. He remained bravely at his post during our rendering of the psalms and hymns, but when we came to the anthem he quietly slunk out with his tail between his legs. When we reached the sermon he returned and dutifully fell asleep.

I think the curate was making use of a sermon he had used that morning at the daughter church, because he seemed to be tying up good churchmanship with a game of golf. And from the expressions on the faces of the congregation, who were still conscious, it was obvious that no one had the faintest idea of what he was driving at.

Interest quickly revived at the end of the sermon. The Sunday was within the octave of one of those obscure Saint's days about which only the vicar had ever heard, and we had a procession. It was the familiar fiasco, dear to the hearts of so many choristers. The boys and girls huddle together and shuffle down the aisle in one glorious discordant mass, followed by the men who straggle, dignified, at a distance, as if to emphasize that they have no connection whatsoever with the firm in front. And at the rear, looking rather embarrassed and singing rather flat, comes the parson.

This particular procession was well on form, and left the congregation wide awake and cheerful. They flowed out of church talking across each other at a tremendous pace and broke up into several animated discussion groups all over the churchyard and the main road. Those on the main road (a courtesy title for the cart track which the parish council were always about to 'do up') were soon obliged to move however. A long sleek cortège of expensive black cars purred slowly past. A man told me it contained the entire congregation of the daughter church on their way home to the fashionable outskirts. The whole thing was most dignified. It was perhaps a little marred by one of the parish churchwardens who drove out of a side road in his veteran paraffin oil delivery van. It got caught up in the middle of the cortège and promptly broke down in a cloud of blue smoke.

It's quite true. Some people are only *fit* for the parish church!

9

Parish Hike

In my teenage days somewhere before the Second World War, hiking was new, exciting and very popular among people of all ages. There was a song, I remember, that everybody knew – 'I'm Happy When I'm Hiking' . . .

Year in, year out, in my home parish the annual parish hike was always endearingly the same. A band of some 30 assorted parishioners assembled at the church hall in the pouring rain, and followed the vicar across the same waterlogged fields, through the same streaming woods, to the same weed-choked disused canal, at the end of which was an ancient barn without a roof where everyone crouched about in corners trying to avoid the worst of the deluge while they munched their sodden sandwiches.

The vicar's warden, who was very conservative in his views, and never failed to write long sad letters of protest to the vicar if he changed a hymn tune or suggested cutting back the belligerent ivy which was forcing its way through the church windows, invariably arrived on the great day attired in a black pin-striped suit, very genteel galoshes and a bowler hat, and carrying a beautifully rolled umbrella which he never opened. And the vicar always came in his great, heather-mixture pullover.

The vicar loved his great hairy, heather-mixture pull-over. He wore it on every possible occasion; in the summer he kept it near him in his study where it sagged over the back of his chair and, for some reason, infuriated the vicarage dog, a delightfully evil-looking mongrel called Ahab, who regularly dragged it down and deposited it in the coal scuttle.

On the occasion when I was inveigled into joining the hike by a formidable rural aunt who, at 85, was the terror of the village street on her tricycle, the weather was no exception to the rule. During the night, a small bridge which was so superbly Regency that for years no one had dared to desecrate it by repairing it, finally got washed away when the rivulet it spanned turned into a raging torrent, and at the other end of the village almost half the choir and all the bell-ringers had narrowly escaped annihilation in the public bar of The Three Goats, where they had been holding a joint meeting about some intolerable grievance or other, when lightning had struck the chimney stack and hurled it through the roof.

But, of course, the hike went on. We moved out across the first field in spanking form with the vicar, a brave figure indeed in his great, hairy, heather-mixture pullover, striding ahead magnificently, and the vicar's warden bringing up the rear, deftly hopping across one puddle into the middle of the next, and discreetly endeavouring to brush the resulting mud spots from his immaculately creased trousers. An angular young lady, sporting what looked like huge, battered football boots and a sort of long policeman's cape, plunged along in the furrow next to mine. 'Invigorating!' she bellowed, slashing at a disheartened-looking cabbage with her walking stick, and neatly filling my turn-ups with water. 'The first time for you, eh? You'll dote on it! You'll come again! *Gets* you, it does. *Gets* you.'

Joyously, she dashed the rain from her face and charged ahead to spur on two elderly gentlemen who were ambling along and talking across each other at an alarming rate. They were, I understood, prominent members of the church council, and hardly ever spoke to each other throughout the year. But they made the annual hike the one exception, and bored each other solidly throughout the entire day with fantasies about their escapades in the Great War.

Some time later, when we had left the fields and were approaching the darkest part of the woods, some of the hikers wanted to take photographs of the party, and we were all lined up in front of a rusty barbed wire fence and a notice which said that trespassers would be prosecuted. The photographers with little automatic cameras clicked at us quickly and barged back eagerly into line, but those with the expensive-looking cameras kept on walking backwards and forwards, and in and out of the trees, and glaring at light meters. Then they all came together in front of us and started shouting entirely contradictory instructions at us as to where we should stand and when we should grin.

A very dedicated artistic-looking young man, hung about with three cameras and quantities of other photographic apparatus in smart little leather cases, presently came up to me with a polite request to get out of the way so that he could take a photograph of himself standing by a small tree which stood on its own, surrounded by an iron railing. He said it had been planted years ago by his grandfather, who had been on the county council, to commemorate some village jollification. He thereupon set up one of his cameras on a tripod, and then rushed to the small tree, stood to attention, and stared grimly into the lens.

But something seemed to be wrong with the mechanism which was supposed to operate the camera automatically after allowing a few seconds for the subject to get into position in front of it. From what I could make out, it persisted in going off too soon and taking pictures of the young man's back. He must have scuttled backwards and forwards between camera and the tree at least half a dozen times before I dared to break into his frantic artistic activity to suggest that perhaps, if he instructed me very carefully, I might be able to take the photograph for him. He appeared very annoyed at this, and said that his photographs appeared in the local paper *and* in the parish magazine and he knew what he was doing.

It was only when I fully realized that I was undermining the whole artistic atmosphere that I also realized that the rest of the party had moved on and were, in fact, wading knee-deep through the wild unspoilt beauty of the stinging nettle beds which grew along the edge of the canal.

I caught up with the rearguard just as they reached the roofless barn at the end of the canal, and by this time it was raining so hard, and the sky was so black, that we could hardly see to unpack our sandwiches in various semi-dry corners. But the vicar stood up, vigorous and encouraging, in a decaying farm cart, and said we needn't worry because he was sure that this was a clearing-up shower, and we should have a fine bright afternoon. In the meantime he would like to draw our attention to a very unusual plant which was growing out of the wall some six feet above where the door of the barn had been. It hadn't been there last year. Could any gardeners in the party say what it was? It looked rather like a lupin, but it wasn't.

The vicar seemed just a little disappointed when there appeared to be no response whatever from the gardeners, not even a wild guess as to what the mysterious lupin-like growth could be. But he cheered up again immediately when the angular young lady in the football boots made a running jump at the wall and started to climb towards the plant.

'No good *gazing* at it,' she panted eagerly over her shoulder. 'Let's get it and examine it.'

The football boots, or some deficiency in her knowledge of climbing a sheer stone wall with no footholds in the pouring rain, prevented her from getting higher than two feet from the ground. Undaunted, however, she suggested that she should stand on the vicar's shoulders, but he said that much as he admired her thorough-going enthusiasm for the job – she really *must* get on to the church council – he reckoned he'd keep a mental picture of the plant, and look it up in a book his wife won at school.

The clearing-up shower kept on clearing-up in torrents until about four o'clock, when we were eventually able to set out on our return journey. The vicar said we didn't want to risk getting bored by covering the same ground twice in one day, so we waded back through an entirely different mass of stinging nettles on the other side of the canal, and across a quite different set of water-logged fields, but we had to go through the same woods because there weren't any others for miles. And it was here that the real thrill of the day came.

The deputy youth club leader (the vicar was the official leader of most of the organizations in the parish, but if you were landed with the actual work you were called a deputy leader) brightly suggested that we should all gather round and have a jolly good sing-song. He'd even remembered his bumper community song book, which he now enthusiastically disentangled from the remains of his corned beef sandwiches and a road map in his haversack.

Quite a number of the hikers didn't seem to hear him and appeared to move on rather hastily, but just then there commenced another clearing-up shower, which promised to be vastly superior to even the fine specimens which we had already experienced. So we all converged under the largest tree in the vicinity, to find that the deputy youth club leader was already there, smiling delightedly at our enthusiasm.

'Now, a good one to start with,' he encouraged, '"Old MacDonald had a farm".' He stood on tiptoe and waved his arms in joyous abandon. 'We all know "Old MacDonald had a farm". Don't we? One. Two. Three . . .'

My formidable rural aunt had tea and crumpets waiting for me when I arrived back after the hike. She didn't seem to mind mud and water all over her dining-room carpet, and she said that getting a little damp wouldn't hurt me at all. She pointed out that if my hair hadn't been so long and untidy my head wouldn't have held so much water, and it wouldn't have run down the back of my neck so much.

'That is the kind of splendid recreation you people in the town *miss*,' she told me, ramming a plate of crumpets on to my sodden knees. 'What would you have been doing with yourself if you hadn't been on our hike? Lounging about in some stuffy, unhealthy picture house, I suppose.'

As she handed me my tea, a large drop of water from my hair splashed neatly into the middle of it, and one of my shoes started to make a curious bubbling sound.

'*Surely* you can see the difference *now*,' she said.

I said I could.

10

Viva Victoria!

I enjoy Victorian church music. No matter what my musical superiors say, I enjoy it. I revel in sugary hymn tunes and anthems that remind one of musical get-togethers following big rugby matches or the Boat Race. I'm so impossible that I see nothing wrong with singing verses about celestial choirs and angels with harps. I even welcome the hymns they sing at football matches. I am, of course, quite beyond the pale and no self-respecting modern church musician would tolerate me.

Luckily for me, however, there still exist some obscure churches where choirs full of Philistines continue to flourish, and in a village in wildest Hampshire I recently found such a haven.

The vicar, whom I met in the church and who gave me permission to sing in the choir that evening, said that there was one most admirable quality about his choir. Unlike so many choirs, they didn't confine their church activities solely to music. Most of them couldn't sing anyway but they did make up for it by serving on the church council and other important committees where they argued for hours.

The service was not due to start for some time, but the choir were already hard at it in the vestry rehearsing a particularly simple anthem with which they were making no progress whatsoever. The organist, I felt, must have been a man of undying faith, for he smiled happily – even a little proudly – at each chaotic onslaught and said it would come in time.

The vicar motioned me to a pew, and we sat down unobtrusively, waiting apparently till 'it' came. In the meantime, I was able to enjoy those surroundings which can only be really appreciated by a chorister who has spent so much of his life in such unique places. There is a strong affinity between most choir vestries. No matter how often the chancel and nave are redecorated or even rebuilt, no one ever seems to notice the state of the choir vestry. You can never say with certainty what colour the distemper was originally supposed to be, and the curtains which mercifully hide the veteran choir robes are traditionally of an indefinable hue, somewhere between grimy green and unwashed blue. If there are any windows, they are heavily stained and discreetly cobwebbed. Two or three dark brown cupboards house some disused flower jars, unused brooms and the music library. If there are any copies that can't be rammed inside the cupboards, they are placed conveniently on top in a mouldering mass. The upper wall space is generally shared between a defunct clock, large enough for a main line railway station, and some reminders of the choir's past glories in the shape of flyblown photos of horse-drawn choir outings.

This vestry boasted all these endearments – and more. Behind the organist of undying faith, I spotted a striking and beautifully decorated notice addressed to the choirboys. It had obviously been executed with such loving care in Victorian days and called the boys' attention to the fines which would be deducted from their pay should they perchance fall short of perfection. Unfortunately the cost of living had necessitated such constant raising of prices and the notice had been altered so many times through the years that it was almost impossible to understand from the mass of figures how much the various shortcomings would now cost you.

However, I could make out some of them. For instance, a fourpenny filthy collar (all the original fines were, of course, in 'old' money) now cost you 50p, and a sixpenny rough-and-tumble set you back £1.50. And whereas you could once have tramped all over the place in gloriously muddy boots for an absolute minimum of threepence, today you couldn't get away with anything under £1.

Presently, while the rehearsal continued on its fruitless and happy way, the more important members of the choir began to arrive for the service. The more important members were those who were very old and never attended rehearsals because they considered it quite unnecessary to waste time practising the same anthems and making the same mistakes which they had made for half a century. As each veteran prepared to robe, he flung his coat flamboyantly across the top of the piano so that by the time everyone was present, the organist, still thumping away regardless, couldn't even see those singers who were still mildly interested in the rehearsal. Finally he smiled again, murmured, 'Splendid effort; jolly good,' and asked the top boy if he'd mind unrolling his copy and not using it as a pea-shooter.

At this point the vicar made me known to the organist, who was so pally that he introduced the choir men using Christian names exclusively. This proved rather confusing, because five of the seven gentlemen concerned were called Charlie. However, the particular Charlie who interested me was, by calling, a gardener who specialized in cutting evergreen shrubs into shapes resembling chickens and horses. He told me he'd been very successful with the shrubs in the churchyard. He'd only one failure. Something had gone wrong with the shape of the shrub outside the vestry door, and everyone said it looked just like the vicar.

So enthusiastic did he become that before I had time to robe he had dragged me outside to admire his handiwork. On a grass patch at the back of the church all kinds of fearsome creatures sprouted from the tortured shrubs, but it was the one that had gone wrong that held me fascinated. It *did* look like the vicar. The more you looked at it the closer the resemblance became. In fact the evergreen vicar delayed us for so long that we forgot the real vicar who had started the service without us.

We robed quickly, and squeezed into the back choir stall. No one noticed us, they were all singing lustily one of those sugary hymn tunes I love so well. The service was what the vicar termed a 'popular' one, which meant that you sang a number of well-known hymns and didn't have to think too much. So I had opportunity to meditate on the vicar's earlier words. Here was a choir who joined in the whole life of the church. What a great deal a choir member can do besides singing – arguing on all the committees, growing chickens and horses in the churchyard . . .

I only hope that some well-meaning vandal doesn't go too far one day and offer to redecorate the vestry.

11

The Down-to-Earth Man

Some months ago I invited myself into the choir of a most charming village church in Dorset where they were having trouble with the lych-gate. It had fallen down.

A friend explained that for years the church council had earnestly and bitterly debated the question of its repair, but in the face of the ultimate disaster, they had rallied to a man, and unanimously agreed that the work should be put in hand immediately. Now they were full of righteous indignation because the local carpenter hadn't called within twelve hours. As the major, who always read the first lesson at Matins, had bellowed to everyone within a hundred yards, it was no wonder we lost contracts to foreigners. When British firms *were* given orders they took half a century to carry them out. But the lych-gate wasn't the only knotty problem which disturbed the serenity of the church council. There were also the questions of the tar up the main aisle and the menace of the new vicar. The tar trouble was a perennial one. The road outside the church was sinking. It sank regularly each summer and, regularly each summer, the authorities sent along some men who slopped tar and sharp little stones all over the place. The sharp little stones never seemed very successful in covering the tar and lay about rather aimlessly. Consequently, on sunny Sundays the congregation unfailingly tramped a most generous coating of tar up the main aisle, and the organist's veteran bike ended up with half a dozen punctures.

And the new vicar was the last straw. He had recently been transferred from a nearby parish where his flock had passed him on, with the greatest relief and a very expensive and utterly tasteless salmon pink clock movingly inscribed with words of deep affection.

He was a large, eager and infuriatingly cheerful type who tackled everybody and everything with the finesse of a steam pile-driver. He was a down-to-earth man and the church council knew exactly where they stood with him. If during a discussion he butted in with 'In my opinion . . . ,' they knew that they still had a slim chance of disagreeing with him; but if he roared 'In my *humble* opinion . . .' they realized that he was dead set on something, and they hadn't a ghost of a chance.

His unique versions of Matins and Evensong were never routine services. They were always part of a campaign for or against something or other, or starting points for special weeks or united efforts. He was particularly fond of united efforts, and these generally concerned such controversial issues that they split the parish from end to end.

At the moment the vicar was full of intense feeling about his latest project. He wanted a new headquarters for the youth club. The members had already wrecked the church room and the village hall, and the vicar felt it was the plain duty of the church to provide them with a much larger and more up-to-date building to wreck. He didn't quite put it like that, of course. His version was that youth needed a more worthy surrounding in which to express their ideals and yearnings unimpeded.

The church council, whose most junior member had recently started to draw his retirement pension, were rather lacking in interest in the whole idea; and the organist, who had to deal with a large amount of the ideals and yearnings of youth in the shape of a dozen and a half delinquent trebles, just laughed a particularly bitter laugh. But nothing could subdue the vicar's dauntless spirit. He blundered on. He said that his most fervent desire was to be *part – really part –* of each and every parish organization.

That is where he immediately fell foul of the choir, who had disliked him since his first Sunday when he had deliberately altered the first hymn tune. He kept on trying to be part of them, and as he couldn't sing a note, and wouldn't even keep quiet, the situation became very explosive. A number of members wrote violent letters of protest to the organist, and even those who couldn't think of anything violent to write added their signatures to other members' efforts. There was a noticeable falling off of attendances at Friday night practices, the more serious singers appearing only when they knew the vicar would be elsewhere offering his humble opinions to some other unfortunates. There were, however, a few stalwarts who continued steadfastly to stick to their posts and never missed a practice. They had a twisted sense of humour, and were curious to see how long the organist could carry on before having a nervous breakdown, resigning, or demanding double salary.

At the time of my visit, heavy rain had followed me from London (it's funny how heavy rain follows me from London) – and although the weather had brightened enough on the Sunday morning to rob any late rising members of the congregation of an excuse for missing Matins, the sun was not strong enough to melt the tar outside the church.

Inside, at the west end, a few anaemic beams picked out a fine Norman pillar, round which was draped a do-it-yourself poster announcing the vicar's latest special effort. It was here that my friend introduced me to the organist. He was obviously a man under a severe strain, but nothing could hide the pride he felt for his small daughter who toddled at his feet. Even as he warmly welcomed me to the choir, his eyes never left her. She had discovered an unusually large and soft heel mark of tar left over from a previous warm Sunday. She was prodding it, gurgling delightedly, and smearing it from top to bottom of her white silk frock . . .

In the vestry I made friends with an extremely large, round, comfortable-looking bass, who was planted happily in everybody's way just inside the door. He was the only choir member on the church council, and he couldn't understand why his fellow councillors had been so edgy of late. True, there were the problems of the lych-gate and the new vicar, but things had a way of settling themselves. In a year or two, someone would have mended the gate, and the vicar would have moved on – a restless type! As for the road outside the church, that would go on sinking, of course, and there would still be tar up the main aisle – but then, there had *always* been tar up the main aisle, so why worry?

12

What Have You Done!

I shall never know how I found the church, because it was miles from the nearest negotiable road, and stood in the middle of a common next to a railway station which had been closed for 40 years. I suppose it would be true to say that my bicycle actually did the discovering. It was one of those tall, dignified, rust-laden models, which are specially preserved by the locals for the use of visitors to English country villages. It had no brakes, which made it very awkward to handle going downhill; but it was even more awkward going uphill, because the chain fell off at the slightest pressure on the pedals.

I couldn't find any level roads, so I decided to give the machine its head, and let it wander unimpeded downhill. It seemed to know its way unerringly through lanes feet deep in mud and stinging nettles, and farmyards full of ferocious ducks and picturesque decaying farm carts. I only had to check its progress once. That was when we came suddenly upon a huge Shire horse, who took up the whole width of the lane, and was so intent on kicking down a drunken-looking fence that he never noticed me, till I dug my heels and pulled up within a few inches of his active hoof.

I admire and am fascinated by Shire horses, but I can never get them to move, and this one was no exception.

So after lifting my bike over a hedge and falling into a ditch, I by-passed him and continued on my way. A few minutes later I found the church. Before I realized what was happening, the bike had come to a sudden halt against a fine eighteenth-century headstone, and deposited me on a pile of broken flower vases.

As I struggled to my feet I became aware of a huge ancient gentleman with a scythe, who looked like a pugilistic version of Old Father Time. He wished me good afternoon most politely, and said that in his opinion my bike would never work again. As he helped me pile it up behind some dustbins of dead flowers, he explained that, besides being the churchyard keeper, he was also the longest-serving member of the choir. When he learned that I, too, was a chorister, we became firm friends, and for the next half hour I couldn't get a word in edgeways. Finally, he announced that he still had a lot of scything to do behind the Indian Mutiny memorial and the potting shed, and left me to explore the church.

It was one of those places that the guide books don't like to mention. It wasn't at all ancient and contained not a single notable work of art, but its Victorian builders had done a splendid job of camouflage. I liked it.

In the choir vestry, I came upon a tall thin gentleman, who was covered with dust and completely surrounded by piles of yellowing music. It stood about in tottering masses all over the piano and on every available chair and form. It thickly covered the floor.

The gentleman smiled at me kindly, and introduced himself as the vicar. Handing me a pile of music which was in an even more advanced state of decay than the rest, he said that he was tidying up the choir music library. 'I've been here nearly two years,' he explained, 'and I still can't find anything. And the trouble is that there isn't anywhere to put everything.' He was therefore trying to re-house neatly all the music in one cupboard instead of the three in which it had been flung for so many years, and thus make room for other essentials which at present evaded him in mysterious hide-outs all over the church. He seemed very pleased to see me, and told me to stand on the bottom of a ladder while he climbed up and emptied another cupboard. In a brisk workmanlike way he handed down stack after stack of music and swept liberal quantities of dirt and plaster all over me. Between fits of choking, I believe I heard him saying something about the choir not using this particular music much these days . . .

He descended the ladder with an armful of sopping wet copies. 'That seems to be the lot,' he announced happily. 'The water tank is up there, and I think it must have overflowed on these . . . And now for the catalogue.'

The catalogue was supposed to list all the music in the library. It was filled with spidery brown writing which had so faded that you couldn't read it, and someone had torn away two dozen pages and half the front cover. A comparatively recent entry at the back stated in bold red pencil that 'Our Kwire master, Old Slater, is a crool beest.'

The vicar's idea was that he should call out the title of the anthem, and that I should find it and place it in the first cupboard. 'I'm *so* glad you came today,' he enthused, regarding my filthy shirt and plaster-covered hair. 'We'll finish this in no time now.'

Quite frankly, I don't know what happened, but two hours later we still hadn't finished. Somehow the music wouldn't go into one cupboard. We couldn't even get it back into the original three cupboards. Indeed we were standing hopelessly beside a mountain of homeless surplus, when the choir man with the scythe reappeared.

He placed his scythe carefully against the wall and gaped at us. 'What have you done?' he asked incredulously. 'What *have* you done?' Trance-like he inspected the two cupboards and then climbed the ladder to the third. He rummaged in it for a few moments and looked down at the vicar. His face was a mask of horror. 'Where's "The Last Judgement" music?' he said. 'It's supposed to be behind the water tank. It's *always* been behind the water tank! What *have* you done?'

As he explained to me later, as I prepared to wash off some of the effects of the afternoon's mischief, 'The vicar's only been here two years. He will *rush* things. You've got to be in a church for *years* to really understand about everything. It comes slowly.'

We were standing in a small room off the vestry. It was crammed with flower vases and handle-less mugs. There was a tap on the wall with no basin under it. I turned the tap gingerly and nothing happened. My friend thumped it smartly with his huge fist and the water flowed immediately. And as it sloshed generously all over my trouser bottoms, I realized how true were his words.

I went to turn off the tap. The tap came away in my hands, and a magnificent fountain of water washed the ceiling for the first time in 50 years.

13

The Lovely Old Dear

The village church where my Uncle Fred is the oldest member of the choir is an ancient pile that you won't find even minutely mentioned in the most comprehensive volumes on ecclesiastical architecture. Uncle Fred says it's the result of 500 years of third-rate jobbing handymen and a complete lack of artistic ability. It's a homely jumble of a building held in great affection by the villagers who, Fred says, would not welcome experts poking around with cameras and note books anyway.

The choir vestry is the most unusual part of the church. It is reminiscent of the interior of a large dilapidated garden shed, with a cobwebbed Gothic window and a part-slate, part-rusting corrugated iron roof. A hefty veteran motor mower half blocks the doorway and a scythe lurks in a dark corner. A sack of fertilizer leans discreetly against the music cupboard and a muddy garden hose and a bundle of spare organ pipes reside behind the vestry piano. And there is, of course, the usual row of pegs and large bent nails from which hang the choir's vestments and an odd disreputable-looking Mac and broken umbrella or two that have been discarded in the pews.

The reason for the vestry's strange association with horticultural aids is an ageless character called Old

Grim. This isn't his real name although certainly he has never been seen to smile. He is the vicarage gardener and general factotum around the church and is also in charge of the churchyard which he keeps in immaculate order down to the last blade of grass. He nurtures whole lists of grudges against everybody and everything but his chief target is the choir. No one really knows why this should be although the popular belief is that, as a boy, he was thrown out of the choir because he was always late for services, never brushed his hair and his boots and was tone deaf. Now he enjoys getting in the way of the choir at every opportunity and is ever full of ideas of how best to do this. Thus the presence of unusual objects in very awkward places in the vestry. But everybody, choir and congregation alike, aver that they really love Old Grim because he has been around in the churchyard even longer than some of the surviving tombstones and is quite irreplaceable at the wage the parochial church council pays him.

So the choir happily continue to put up with Old Grim and Old Grim quite happily continues to devise ways of getting in the way of the choir and the choir vestry remains the unique place it has always been as the centre of the parish's musical activities. These consist of the choir meeting every Friday evening ostensibly for the purpose of rehearsing the music for Sunday, but actually to spend most of the time sitting around exchanging the latest gossip on improvised seats including the fertilizer sack and various tea chests containing the choir's 'library' of music that hasn't seen the light of day for decades. Then towards the end of the period the organist, a spare, middle-aged, dandified bachelor, a happy man always gushingly friendly and encouraging to everyone in the choir, suggests lightly that they might look at the hymns and psalms and the anthem for Sunday. Everyone knows these and has sung them (disastrously, according to Old Grim) for years and years so the 'looking at' doesn't take more than a few minutes and the organist accordingly closes proceedings with assurances such as, 'Well, yes it goes something like that – but it'll go all right on Sunday'.

And everyone retires to The Goat and Compasses safe in the knowledge that if it doesn't go right on Sunday, the choir's principal soprano, a truly delightful girl with a delightful voice, can be depended on to fill in with a solo at a minute's notice.

The wildly unlikely fact is that the delightful soprano is the granddaughter of Old Grim – and naturally Old Grim disagrees with her being in the choir, 'wasting your time with that bunch of incompetents'. But this doesn't worry her in the least and she always says he's her favourite man and that if others in the parish had been active church members for half as long as he has and had had to put up with the dozens of odd vicars with scores of odd ideas about how to run the parish that he has, they would tend to go a bit strange too, but actually her granddad is a lovely old dear.

And at the time of my recent visit to Uncle Fred the lovely old dear was exercising the minds of the church officials rather more than usual. Fred explained that some busybody on the parochial church council had discovered by chance that Old Grim's eightieth birthday was approaching and so, at the next meeting of the council, in line with the parish's official warm community image of everyone loving Old Grim, the members immediately and wholeheartedly agreed that something special must be done to celebrate his birthday, as long as none of them had to do it. Accordingly, they promptly bequeathed the job to the organist who had a name for being such a pleasant person who was always so full of enthusiasm about everything, even the choir, and could get blood out of a stone.

As the organist and choir had most contact with Old Grim by way of putting up with maliciously placed lawn mowers and scythes and sacks of fertilizer, they willingly took on the assignment, and as an honorary member of the choir I found myself present at the meeting called to start the ball rolling. It was a cold November Sunday evening after Evensong and the vestry heating, having broken down as usual (Old Grim was supposed to 'see to it' but he always said he was a gardener, not a heating engineer, and no one ever seemed to have an answer to that), we all sat around a large fuming oil stove and stared at the organist who carefully spread a red silk handkerchief on the sack of fertilizer and settled himself comfortably. 'Well,' he bounced the question at us, 'what do we do for the old —,' and realizing too late that the subject's granddaughter was present as a member of the choir, '— what do we do for the old gentleman?'

Three identical-looking basses – large, round, red-faced and black suited, hunched precariously on the music library tea chests – growled together for some moments before their spokesman boomed, 'What about getting him a new motor lawn mower? The old one's been falling to bits for years and it makes such an awful smell.'

'Oh, for heaven's sake!' exploded a very important-looking contralto lady next to me who normally kept aloof from idle chatter in the choir and only spoke in definitive pronouncements to illustrate her superior knowledge of the subject. She shot out a substantial arm across my face, aiming an admonishing bejewelled finger at the three basses. 'What a stupid suggestion! If he gets another great big lawn mower we shan't be able to get into the vestry at all. He'll park it next to the old one in the doorway and ... Oh! ... For heaven's sake.'

The three basses took no notice of her in the same way that they take no notice of her when they are singing in the choir. With her exclusive parade-ground voice she is always striving to move things along, while the basses savour every note, always ignore her, and rumble along behind at their own dignified pace leaving the rest of the choir to take sides, or follow the vicar, who also has an exclusive parade-ground voice but doesn't always know the tune.

The gathering now appeared to realize, however, that if the subject of the meeting had incited the very important-looking contralto to condescend to give voice it was indeed a serious meeting, so everyone switched on expressions of deep, thoughtful concern and sat tight, waiting for someone else to make the next move. No one did, for what seemed an age during which time the vicar put his head round the door, wished us well in our deliberations and sidled off swiftly to his supper, while from the churchyard bellowed the 'lovely old dear' vowing to annihilate a late lingering choirboy who'd stepped on the grass.

But, truth to tell, the majority of Fred's choir don't have much to say at choir meetings unless discussing the next summer outing or the Christmas binge at The Goat and Compasses. This meeting floundered on for a full hour and despite the enthusiastic beams from the organist it seemed that no further suggestions would be forthcoming about Old Grim's eightieth birthday. Members passed round and round a plate of soggy biscuits left over from the vicar's last coffee morning and either politely accepted second cups of a motherly choir lady's transparent cold tea ('Well, the meeting started late and I had the tea ready early') or bravely refused to have anything to do with it. Finally, unexpectedly, a bright, birdlike little lady, who can read music and turns the pages of the organist's music when he is raging through the voluntary after Matins, rose shyly, and suggested that would it not be a good idea to buy Old Grim a big garden shed for the churchyard so that he could accommodate all his implements together and thus leave the vestry clear for the choir?

Someone said 'Splendid' and started to clap. There and then the tension relaxed. The whole parish would be mightily relieved. The organist's enthusiasm knew no bounds. His reputation for being able to get blood out of stones would be vindicated to the hilt.

A splendid large sum of money resulted in a splendid large garden shed being erected in the churchyard and everyone was so overjoyed that Old Grim accepted it –

well, as Uncle Fred said, although he complained about nosy parkers who unearthed his birthday date, he didn't actually refuse to use the new shed.

Weeks later – on Christmas Eve in fact – I was again making my way to Uncle Fred's church, this time to sing in the choir at the Midnight Service. At the lych-gate I was delighted to fall in with Old Grim's ever-charming granddaughter, the choir's face-saving soprano soloist. 'Come with me,' she said, and she led the way through the churchyard to the splendid new shed. The door was padlocked but in the bright moonlight we could see clearly through the windows. The shed was crammed, bulging, overflowing. 'How right it was,' I said. She regarded me with dancing eyes. 'He loves his shed.'

We moved on to the vestry. I pushed the door open for her. A hefty veteran motor mower blocked the way, a scythe lurked behind. Members of the choir were stepping around a large sack of fertilizer leaning against the music cupboard. She paused in the doorway, looking at me anxiously. 'He works so hard,' she murmured. 'He's so enthusiastic . . . He's such a lovely old dear.' She was very beautiful standing there in the moonlight. 'He is,' I heard myself saying, 'I'm sure he is.'

14

Have Your Say!

We'd been vaguely in touch but I hadn't actually seen Jack, an old bachelor chorister friend, since he retired from City life and moved to what he expected to be serener pastures midst gentle acres of Suffolk, six years ago. Then, recently, still vaguely, Jack thought it would be a pleasant idea if I came along to look over his happy hide-away. So today we had just met at a small, quite charming rural railway station, which was, remarkably, still in working order, the nearest public transport point to Jack's village, and were now meandering along lumpy lanes and secret cart tracks in his stout little horse box. ('I use it for everything except my horse – he prefers to walk.')

Jack, who had joined the village church choir within days of arriving in the village, was talking of country parish life and the goings on at the church, which, like the station, was still in good working order. 'We are a traditional country parish here,' he told me comfortably. 'We all know how to deal with each other without kicking up a fuss.' I said that these days it seemed hard to decide what a traditional country parish actually was – what with clergy shortages and only one church service a month and closed post offices and no organists, and hymns having to be called songs.

'Oh, we're the traditional sort of traditionalists here,' he assured me – 'easily managed old vicar (firmly 'advised' by his wife in everything), choir and organist who more or less run the show on Sundays, church council who never agree on anything at meetings and thoroughly enjoy arguing for hours and ending up playing darts in The Goat and Compasses. Life goes on cheerfully,' Jack chuckled. 'The vicar *did* overdo it a bit a week ago, though. He was illustrating to a wavering parishioner how, if you decide it is right to do something, like actually walking 150 yards to church on Sunday morning instead of using the car or getting a hymn tune changed in the face of the organist's entrenched wishes, you can be victorious against all odds – if you have faith. He was up a ladder cleaning out an awkwardly placed guttering over the church porch at the time and the waverer was admiring his determination. Then the ladder slipped and the vicar fell and broke a leg.' Jack smiled reassuringly at my look of concern. 'Oh, he'll be all right. His wife had decided that apart from his broken leg, the vicar needs an extended break from his parish duties, so next week she is taking him on a holiday in the Austrian alps.'

'Austrian alps – with a broken leg?' I queried.

'Oh, yes,' he maintained matter-of-factly. 'The vicar's wife is a not inconsiderable figure in the parish. You can't miss her (however much you try). She has the firmest, often most profound views and unworkable ideas about everything and everybody and has such a charming, encouraging way – the vicar's warden calls it a sort of spiritually overbearing bullying – of laying down the law that even the most formidable trouble makers on the church council don't get involved with her if they can help it. The power behind the throne y'see.'

'And the vicar?' I queried.

'He respects authority,' he said.

'Would you say, then, that as far as the congregation are concerned, the whole organization in your parish is unusually autocratic for these days?' I asked. Jack shook his head vigorously and beamed. 'Good heavens, no! Nothing like that. Parishioners have their say all right – they may not get their way, but they have their say. Their favourite pastime is rubbishing the choir. It's a sort of rustic tradition here from the eighteenth century when the choir were an uncouth rabble shoved out of sight in the gallery.'

'Well, your choir must have improved their image since then,' I suggested.

'No! Not in the eyes of the vicar's wife,' he assured. 'Her oft repeated view is that years ago the uncouth rabble were at least hidden in the gallery whereas today they are in the chancel in choir stalls in full view of everybody.' I supposed I looked a little apprehensive. Jack smiled a cheerful, encouraging smile. 'Oh, there's nothing to worry about . . . Our choir are like the Crimean war general's tomb in the churchyard. Its huge belligerent mass of grimy marble covered with swooping black angels partially blocks the path to the church porch and has inadvertently featured largely in hundreds of wedding photos of the arrival of the bride. Well, nobody's going to shift the general's tomb – or our choir! We're tradition, y'see.'

Presently we arrived in the stable yard at the back of Jack's sturdy little red-brick house. As we clambered out of the horse box a knowing-looking horse of the Shire variety snorted a welcome from his open stable and plodded towards us. We both made a fuss of him and Jack said his name was Samson but no one called him Samson because on the day he arrived the vicar's wife had fallen in love with him as soon as she saw him and announced that his name was to be the saintly sounding Francis.

I began to wonder about the vicar's wife – the vicar's power behind the throne? Over tea, Jack spoke affectionately of her. 'She's very good at getting people to *do* things – knows what she wants and when. She's got a *presence*, a very *imposing* presence – a statuesque lady with swirling dresses and a big melodious voice. At parish parties and summer fetes she sort of *flows* to the centre of things and envelops people and you find yourself saying yes to her, almost before she's finished outlining the task she wants you to tackle.

In the churchyard a few dozen paces along the village street from Jack's house the postcard-pretty church seemed to be leaning gently against two magnificent oaks, mighty sentinels that had obviously stood there ages before the arrival of the Victorian builders.

As we reached the vestry door the lady herself billowed forth, obviously in a great and important hurry. She stopped abruptly, however, as we hastily stood aside for her. 'You'll do, Jack,' she announced to my friend. 'I can't find the organist anywhere. Here is the list of hymns the vicar wants for the service that I've chosen.' Jack replied smartly that he'd pass the list to the organist as soon as he arrived – he expected he was late because he'd been having trouble with his veteran motor bike lately and this tended to make him very uptight and affected his organ playing and the choir members he shouted at – and this was an old friend from Richmond (the Surrey one) who was going to help out in the choir this morning ...

Jack had to speak very quickly, blending one item with the next as the lady was already on the move again. She beamed at me momentarily over her shoulder and said I was very welcome as she disappeared through the back entrance to the vicarage. Her large melodious voice drifted back to us, reporting to the vicar that all was in readiness for the service, except the organist who was apparently having some further trouble with his awful bike – and some of the choir people of course who, poor dears, were never on time or in tune.

Actually, the entire choir had turned up in time to process into the chancel for Choral Matins as the organist blundered into the organ box at the last minute, producing a few triumphant introduction chords. Then all went well with the familiar procedure and well-known hymns, with the vicar with his leg in plaster safely installed in his place at the head of the choir stall, valiantly keeping up with the choir's tearaway pace and exuberant volume. In no time at all, it seemed, we had reached the point in the service when the week's notices were announced. Jack explained in a hoarse whisper, 'We can relax for a bit now. This is where the vicar reads out the marriage banns and all kinds of other stuff. Then he asks the congregation if there is any other matter that anybody wants to raise and everyone is so keen and committed that they all speak at once and nobody can hear what anybody is saying but it doesn't matter because they say the same things week after week and over time the great ideas and the grouses gradually get through to the vicar because his wife pieces everything together and summarizes for him with her added guidance on what his reactions should be – she's very good at summarizing and guiding.'

Jack paused, a little breathless, giving me time to comment. 'And all this goes on during Choral *Matins*?' I queried.

'Oh, yes,' Jack sounded confident, quite proud. 'Our Choral Matins is not just any old service, you know. It's alive, challenging, dedicated – there are some parishioners who are so dedicated that they bring their demands and things on slips of paper which they hand in as they arrive for the service. It saves them doing all that shouting. There's a man who's been sending in requests for months for a new boot scraper outside the church porch because the path round the Crimean general's tomb is so muddy on wet days. And there's half a dozen people who want the choir sacked and recorded hymns played from the choir stalls.'

I didn't have to wonder what the choir did while all the activity was going on in the nave. Jack indicated a number of choristers quietly reading their Sunday papers and others just quietly studying the ceiling. 'Y'see, as a matter of principle, we don't get involved,' Jack explained.

'And might that be something to do with the congregation always rubbishing the choir?' I speculated. Jack chuckled gently.

'The choir are part of the rich historical fabric of our parish, the vicar says it every year at the choir dinner. If ever they disappeared or merely stopped singing like they do, it would be disastrous. The congregation would have to find some other lot to rubbish. The whole life of the parish would be derailed. Anyway,' he brightened, that's never likely to happen. You should see the size of the congregation on "Thank you Choir" Sunday when parishioners have the opportunity of showing their appreciation of the choir. I tell you they are blocking the aisles and hanging from the rafters. The choir sings their favourite anthems – all very rumbustious Victorian affairs with lovely slushy solos and then the vicar thanks the choir with real over-the-top expressions of delight and asks what would we do without them. Nobody attempts to answer that question openly and everybody puts a lot of money into the collection for the choir's annual outing and all go home happy and invigorated. And no one rubbishes the choir for at least a fortnight. It's our wonderful tradition, y'see.'

That evening Jack saw me off home from the attractive railway station which was still in working order and there was a twinkle in his eye. 'I've got an idea you wouldn't mind helping us again in the choir quite soon,' he said. How right he was! What a lovely parish he'd found – a cheerfully united church where constantly more than a few differing views and attitudes, however unfulfilled, were happily put up with and a great flow of humour was always around, all resulting, amongst other things, in a rattling good service on Sunday. How human. How C of E!

15

Lead, Kindly Light

In a delightful unspoilt country town where some buses still have conductors I saw, the other day, one of those gentlemen who stand about in shop doorways, and seem to be counting buses. They carry large note-pads on which they keep making little ticks, and they all appear to dress in long raincoats, pulled-down hats, and crumpled white scarves. No one ever takes any notice of them, and they ignore everything except the buses, which they tick off without even looking up. When the evening rush-hour queues start forming at the bus stops, they suddenly produce incredibly ancient bikes from alleyways and front garden hedges, and quietly ride away.

The bus counters in this town had to detect quite a large number of buses. Three separate companies operated services to the smaller town where I was spending a brief holiday, but they all took different routes. The first one took the shortest, most direct route. This lay right through the centre of the town, which had been designed for the smooth passage of pony traps and penny-farthing bicycles. Whatever time of the day or night you travelled, the bus always got caught up in the permanent bottle-neck at the end of the High Street caused by the belligerent intrusion of a huge black statue of a past town councillor, who was never happy unless he was in the public eye.

The second route avoided the town centre, and travelled round a maze of mysterious back streets which seemed to consist solely of second-hand clothes shops, pubs, fried fish bars, broken gas lamps, and houses without front gardens. There was little to delay the buses on this route, save the occasional rag-and-bone cart or beer dray, but it was such a long way round that it took as much time as the bottle-necked route.

The third route was most extraordinary. It eventually got you to the next town, but, before doing so, it very cleverly wound itself back on its own tracks, and ten minutes after you'd boarded the bus you found yourself back where you'd started. Moreover, the buses on this route didn't always turn up, and now and again those that *did* would rush past the stops and only pull up in the middle of a traffic jam where you couldn't get off.

No one seemed to know why this should be, but I believe it had something to do with shortage of staff and tea breaks. Anyway, the best thing to do was to catch the first bus you came across and hope for the best.

The bus I eventually caught (and it needed some catching because it was one of those on which the conductor watches you running frantically until you are within a dozen yards of the platform, and then leans heavily on the bell-push) was on the fried fish and pub route, and we were soon sailing along unimpeded through the unspoilt hideousness of the Industrial Revolution. A large panting gentleman, who had been struggling up the gangway with two long string bags overflowing with shopping, came violently to rest on the seat next to mine, as the bus lurched round a blind corner between a brewery and a gas works. A mud-splattered cabbage, an outsized pair of steel-tipped boots, and a bottle of vinegar fell out of one of the bags on to my lap, and he said he was very sorry, and would I just shove 'em back while he held the bag open. He kindly smeared the mud from the cabbage a little farther over my raincoat with a large off-white handkerchief, and after that, of course, we started talking.

It transpired that he lived very near where I was staying and was, indeed, a bass in the church choir in which I hoped to sing on the following Sunday. He was most enthusiastic. In no time at all, he was telling me all about the members of the choir. There was a man who regularly ruined the responses by hanging on to the last one for six beats longer than anyone else, and there was another man who sang the soprano line in a thunderous bass voice. There was also an ancient character who insisted on singing all the tenor solos, although his voice had left him 20 years ago, and there was a Welshman who, for some obscure reason, favoured plaid socks and a cassock which hardly reached below his knees. The vicar always spoke kindly to the choirmen in the vestry on Sundays, and always tried to hurry past when he ran into them streaming out of The Three Loggerheads on Saturdays. The organist was 82 years old, and lived with an even older sister who had never let him marry because she said it wasn't fair to *any* girl.

All this I learned before we had reached the halfway point in our journey. After the bus had been at a standstill for 25 minutes outside a very ornate undertaker's establishment, and the driver and conductor had disappeared, my bass companion broke off his narrative to explain that this kind of delay did sometimes occur. They changed bus crews here, he said, and it might be ages before we got moving again. He said that the local papers had been full of complaints for years and the question was regularly raised in the council chamber. For as far back as he could remember, all the local election candidates had *sworn* to do something about it. He believed the bus company was looking into the matter.

He suggested that our best way was to walk down to the public baths where we could pick up another bus which would get us home more quickly. We tramped a good half mile to the public baths, a nightmare of terracotta tiles and top heavy, onion-like domes. For the last quarter of a mile there had been a most unexpected cloudburst, and as we waited, bus-less and drenched, beneath one of the biggest onions, our original bus roared across the top of the road. The large bass said the crew must have turned up earlier than expected. That was always a risk you had to take ...

He took me along to the church on Sunday morning. In his little guide to the building, the vicar had rather gallantly written: 'The present church is the product of many generations of dedicated craftsmen and artists.' What he really meant was that, whenever they had wanted to add a new porch, or vestry, or memorial chapel, the local builder had knocked a big hole in the church wall and stuck it on. Consequently the church now presents the homely battered appearance which has so endeared it to a large and faithful congregation. Indeed, it attracts the faithful from considerable distances outside its own parish, and they arrive unerringly Sunday after Sunday. True, they arrive at all sorts of odd times. Owing to the lack of car parks the three bus services are always in great demand. Over a cup of coffee in the church hall after service, the outlying faithful entertain each other with their latest fantastic stories of how their particular bus got them to church half an hour before the church opened, or during the last chaotic chords of the anthem, or halfway through the sermon. The local faithful are no less interested, and crowd round eagerly. A most entertaining discussion follows.

Only one person seems completely disinterested in the whole thing. He is the man in the choir who regularly ruins the responses by hanging on to the last one for six beats longer than anyone else. Immediately the service is over he mounts his ancient bicycle and rides away. During the week he dresses in a long raincoat, pulled-down hat and crumpled white scarf. He stands in doorways and makes little ticks on a large note-pad . . .

16

A Heavy Responsibility

When you are staying as a guest in the house of a friend, it is always rather difficult to decline to fall in with his suggestions of how you should spend your time. For some days I had explored the small Gloucestershire town and its surroundings, quite unimpeded, but on this particular morning my friend asked me if I'd like to help him do some moving. He wanted to lift some discarded choir stalls on to a coal lorry.

'They're solid oak,' he said, 'and they weigh *tons* and *tons*. They've been in the builder's yard ever since he took them out of the old chapel in the High Street – you know, the one that's been turned into a Bingo Hall.' He rubbed his hands together in pleasurable anticipation of a morning's brisk hard work. 'Those choir stalls haven't been touched for *years*,' he assured me. 'They're absolutely *filthy*. We'll have to clean them up before we move them. And of course we'll have to sweep up the coal lorry a bit.'

Now, quite frankly, I have never felt any great urge to lift filthy choir stalls weighing tons and tons on to either swept or unswept coal lorries, but in the circumstances I said I'd be delighted. After all, as my friend pointed out, it was for a jolly good cause.

The jolly good cause was the annual carnival procession. This year the parish church was entering a float, and the idea of the choir stalls was entirely due to the vicar's brainwave. Some of the choir members who didn't like new ideas said it must have been more like a brain storm; but then, they didn't understand much about publicity. Anyway, it was well known that the vicar would try anything once, and he'd often try it more than once, especially if no one else wanted it. His present idea was to have the church choir actually standing in the choir stalls and singing Old English songs, interspersed with organ music played on a tape-recorder concealed behind a dummy organ. Actual details about the completion of the float were a bit vague, but they had something to do with draping the coal lorry with flags and imitation grass, and pictures of the graveyard before and after the removal of the gravestones. There was also going to be a churchwarden sitting on the tail-board, giving away copies of the parish magazine that hadn't been sold on the previous Sunday.

When my friend and I reached the builder's yard, we found the vicar already in charge. He was pacing up and down, rarin' to go, a large, moon-faced, hearty man, with a voice that made it utterly impossible for the churchwardens in the back pew to doze off during the sermon. He kindly gave us a broom each, and set us to work on the discarded choir stalls. There didn't seem to be a broom for him, but he didn't complain. While we concentrated on our job, he examined the coal dust on the lorry and worked out the most efficient method of getting rid of it. As is usually the case, this was the most simple and straightforward method, and merely entailed my friend and I transferring our brooming efforts from the choir stalls to the lorry, while the vicar directed and encouraged us from a respectable distance.

After an hour or so of good hard work, everything was reasonably clean, and the vicar said we'd done a good job, and roared with laughter at my blackened shirt. ('Nearly as black as some of the choir surplices! Ha! Ha!') He said we'd only have to give the stalls a good polish now and they'd look like new again. But first we'd get them up on the lorry. No good polishing them and then covering them with our black finger-marks!

Somehow I dragged myself on to the lorry and clutched at the end of a stall. I couldn't move it an inch. Of course, that is where my inexperience showed. As soon as the vicar explained to me how to hold the thing, and instructed my friend how to lift the other end, it was much easier and, after only a dozen attempts, we had it balancing on the tail-board. The vicar applauded, 'Splendid! Jolly good!' and told my friend that it only wanted one good hefty shove to put it in place. I must admit he urged us on very well, and if we'd been a tug-o'-war team I'm sure we'd have won against the most tremendous odds, but somehow my friend had not quite mastered the art of doing the work of six men because he suddenly seemed to lose interest and made as if to fall down. But the vicar was there with his good hefty shove. It succeeded magnificently and drove me from one end of the lorry to the other where I ended up, with the breath knocked out of me, between the end of the stall and the driving cab.

Success is a great stimulant. It only remained for us to lift the end of the other stall on to the lorry, and the job would be nearly done. The vicar said he was sure we'd be all right now that we'd got the hang of the thing, and he was just going to pop round to the shop which was supplying the flags and imitation grass. He'd also bring back a tin of polish, so that we could make a really first-class job of the stalls . . .

Deprived of the vicar's encouragement, we were rather slower in the placing of the second stall but, apart from a few minor injuries, we managed it very well, and our noisy gasping for breath was gradually subsiding as the vicar returned. He tossed us a two pound tin of polish and some nice new dusters. A really *vigorous* polishing was what was necessary, he said. And while we were doing that, he'd pin up the decorations. It was, after all, the decorations which made or marred a float. He draped some mauve muslin right across the driving mirror and stood back to view it with evident delight and satisfaction.

Only one defect caused the vicar the smallest uncertainty about the superiority of the parish church float. The man who had made the dummy organ had made it a foot or so too wide for the coal lorry, and we couldn't use it. But, as usual the vicar saved the day. He drove the lorry round to the vicarage, and very kindly allowed us to load his own piano on to it. As we dragged it on to the tail-board, he stood back and gazed at it with pride. He said they didn't make pianos like that these days. It was solid mahogany – had a good iron frame . . .

The carnival procession that evening was a great success. We watched it from my friend's front bedroom, where we lay propped up with cushions. The vicar, a brave imposing figure, stood on the parish float, baton in hand, as he waited to conduct the choir in their Old English songs. But I understand that by the end of the procession he was looking just a little annoyed. The float had been followed directly by the town brass band, and they simply would *not* stop playing 'Colonel Bogey'.

17

The Contralto Lady

There aren't many good male alto singers in church choirs these days. In fact, the situation must have been pretty desperate for years in some places. I sing a sort of alto, and in our choir they've put up with me quite uncomplainingly for as long as I can remember. And normally, whenever I visit a choir and announce that I am an alto, I am given a really warm welcome.

But at the Wiltshire village church which I recently revisited, I think I was rather a mixed blessing. As soon as I made my appearance in the vestry for Sunday Evensong, the choirmaster almost fell on my neck, and started violently shaking my hand and thumping my shoulder.

'Splendid! Splendid!' he enthused. '*So* glad to see you again.' He reached for a copy of the evening's anthem – a well-known pot-boiler by S. S. Wesley – and he insisted that I should take part in the quartet. 'You really *must* do it,' he urged. 'I'm sure our usual lady contralto won't mind standing down. After all, we see you so seldom.'

But remembering their usual lady contralto, I was very sure that she *would* mind. She lived in shapeless home-spun tweeds and large gaping brogue shoes, and always took part in *all* the quartets, and always completely drowned and flattened the other three voices.

In fact, I have a strong suspicion that the choirmaster's eagerness for me to sing had nothing to do with any curious beauty in my voice, but was because it is a very unobtrusive voice and, when up against a good soprano, is almost inaudible. He was simply seizing an opportunity of warding off a nerve-wracking experience.

I started to decline gracefully, and then frantically, as I saw the lady in question sail into the vestry and bear down on us. But the choirmaster steeled himself and blundered on. Quickly moving behind the piano, he greeted her with a dutiful smile.

'Of course, you remember our friend,' he introduced me. 'I was just telling him that you wouldn't mind at all letting him have a go at the quartet tonight.'

The lady contralto replied sweetly that of *course* she didn't mind, and I sensed the choirmaster wilting under her glare. But he had won a point and, as he climbed into the organ loft, I saw a smile of relief on his face.

Unfortunately, by this time, I had developed a most annoying toothache which gave the unmistakable impression that it was likely to go on for hours. And another member of the quartet, an attractive soprano who, during my previous visit, had taken me to see the surrounding countryside in a fiendish red sports car and had driven so fast that I hadn't seen anything at all, noticed the pained expression on my face and tried to cheer me up by assuring me that I need not be afraid of the lady contralto because her bark was worse than her bite, poor dear. When, however, she learned the true reason for my discomfort, she gave me one of her most delightful smiles and offered me an aspirin. She said that in the case of toothache it often helped if you took an aspirin and filled your mind with restful, serene thoughts.

I took the aspirin, but somehow the restful, serene thoughts seemed to be keeping clear of that vestry. However, the rest of the choir were most friendly and accommodating. The only trouble was that, when we took up our places in the choir stalls, I discovered that no one had provided me with a copy of the anthem. The tenor next to me explained that they were rather short of copies, and we should have to look three over a copy. He said that they always looked three to a copy when they did this one – except the lady contralto. She always had one to herself.

On this particular evening the psalm was a short one and the vicar, who had his eye on two choirboys who were playing miniature chess under the book rest, forgot to announce one of the hymns, so the anthem was on us before we realized it. The tenor next to me and the bass on his other side reverently held before us a much patched copy which threatened to disintegrate at any moment. The bass was a member of the quartet, but the tenor wasn't. For some reason, the quartet-tenor was on the other side of the chancel, half hidden behind a pillar against which he leaned most gracefully.

And, all things considered, I think we sang very well. I couldn't hear what the tenor behind the pillar was singing, or if he was singing at all, but the bass and the soprano didn't overdo things and, now and again, I could distinctly hear myself. I wasn't surprised to note the expression of agony on the face of the lady contralto as she carefully examined the ceiling, but I must confess I was a little puzzled by the tenor who was sharing our copy. He kept muttering 'Good heavens! *Good* heavens…!'

Nevertheless, I still felt quite happy about things – until we were approaching the end of the quartet.

The choirmaster had stressed the absolute necessity of singing softly here, exactly as marked by Wesley. But I don't think Wesley had in mind noisy vicars when he composed that anthem, for it was now that the vicar started clumping his dignified way from the chancel to the pulpit, so that he could break into his sermon before the last note of the anthem had died away. He had a loose metal tip on one of his shoes and it clicked, loudly and completely out of time with our singing, on the brass plaques full of pious remarks about bygone parishioners which covered the floor.

After Evensong, we all stood about talking in the churchyard and by this time my tooth, which had quite disregarded the aspirin, was thumping like a particularly powerful steam-hammer. Presently, the lady contralto again bore down on me.

'Bad toothache, eh?' she bellowed. 'Probably brought on by *tension*, y'know. When you're not used to singing solo parts, it *does* affect the nerves sometimes.' She said that it was most unfortunate that this should happen on a Sunday when no dentists were available as, of course, it would mean that I should have to go *right* through the night with the *wretched* pain, and would certainly get no sleep at all. She explained that I would feel like a wet rag in the morning, and in no fit state to even *see* a dentist. She assured me that she was very sorry indeed, and she smiled consolingly with a large false-toothy smile.

Then suddenly, from behind the church, a fiendish red sports car hurled itself to a screeching halt at the churchyard gate. I knew it well. Through the cloud of dust and petrol fumes, the attractive soprano leaned out and called to me. Apparently her uncle, who lived in a nearby town, was a dentist and a 'dear old thing' who would do anything for her. I was to come with her and get rid of my tooth *immediately*.

I got into the car obediently. I didn't look back to see if the lady contralto was still smiling.

18

A Beautiful Woman with
Ruffled Hair

I admire paddle-steamers. And the one which was approaching the seaside jetty where I stood surrounded by a mob of choirboys and a handful of reluctant grown-up 'helpers' was most admirable. Heavy black smoke billowed from her stack and curled forward in the lazy summer breeze, giving her the uninhibited appearance of a beautiful woman with ruffled hair. She was a magnificent sight.

At least, that is what I thought, but a choirboy who stood near me didn't see it my way at all. He was a large prickly haired urchin with a particularly round and happy face. He regarded the steamer aghast.

'D'yer mean ter say we're going on that blinking old tub?' he demanded with the full force of his lungs above the chaotic uproar. 'Looks to me as though it's going to sink any minute. Looks as though the bottom's going to drop out. Talk about Noah's Ark! I bet Noah wouldn't have risked his neck in *that*. I bet…' But I never heard what else he bet, because the choirmaster suddenly appeared from nowhere. He requested the young gentleman to kindly refrain from bothering me with derogatory remarks about a very fine ship, otherwise he would have no alternative but to clout his unkempt, stupid, thick head. And he removed him from under my elbow with an expert grip on the scruff of his neck.

The choirboys' annual outing, which traditionally included a steamer trip, was a terrifying experience for all its organizers except the choirmaster, a tall lean man, who had somehow endeared himself to generations of choirboys, and was the most cynical person I'd ever met. He watched the near riot as the steamer drew alongside and his charges surged forward to throw orange peel and empty ice-cream cartons into the gilded paddle-box.

'Careful! You might fall into the water and get churned up by the paddle-wheel,' he called hopefully.

The boys squeezed up the gang-plank in a roaring mass – all except little Anthony who, accompanied by his Mama, followed at a safe distance. Little Anthony spoke beautifully, was always raising his cap, and agreed with his Mama that his colleagues were rude, rough, naughty boys. He had joined the choir because his Mama wanted him to take advantage of the choirmaster's splendid (and free) musical training, but he never mixed with the other boys. He was, moreover, very conscientious, and often reported them to the choirmaster when he happened to come upon them acting in a rude, rough manner. Lately he had begun to think his efforts in this direction were in vain because the choirmaster never seemed to do much about his reports, and he wondered whether a direct approach to the vicar might not be more fruitful...

Within a few seconds of boarding, the boys had crushed themselves into the microscopic space under the saloon stairs which always seems to be set aside in paddle-steamers for the refreshment bar. Those of the other passengers who could escape did so promptly, and those who were trapped flattened themselves against the walls, and held aloft their tea and stale cakes until they were swept out of their hands. A large comfortable-looking man near me, whose tea had been upset right down the front of his wife's new dress, summoned a Christian smile and said that boys would be boys, and that it was all harmless fun, and that they looked a jolly, healthy, good-hearted lot of lads anyway.

Soon, the glorious smell of mingled oil and steam drew the mob away from the refreshment bar to the engine-room where boys, young and ancient, always gather to watch those mighty labouring piston-rods as they plunge and climb, and turn the churning paddles. Mesmerized, forgetful of time and appetite, they lolled over the protecting partition, their iced lollies melting unheeded down each other's necks. Only momentarily were they recalled from their paradise by the choirmaster, who later bore down on them, blowing clouds of evil-smelling smoke from a battered pipe.

'Ah! Enjoying ourselves, I see,' he beamed. 'Taking full advantage of the sun and sea air!'

He passed on under his canopy of smoke, leaving me alone with the mob. (The other 'helpers', as was their respected custom, were up on deck, well hidden behind the funnel.) By chance, the large happy urchin of earlier acquaintance was again at my elbow. He grinned hugely at me. I grinned back.

'It's a pity the vicar couldn't be here today,' I said foolishly. He transferred a melting bar of chocolate from one filthy fist to the other. He thought for a moment.

'Well, we don't really mind him,' he admitted. He grinned even more hugely. 'But we like the organ-grinder the best – that man with the pipe. He's *jolly* good. He can think up the most *rude* things to call people – you ought to hear what he calls us at choir practice. He thinks of something different every week. He's *jolly* good.'

As the cruise neared its end, the mob had drifted back round the refreshment bar under the stairs. The choir-master and his pipe had rejoined us, and we could now only just discern each other through the fog. The ancient mariner in charge of the bar was telling us that the steamer company had recently tried to persuade him to transfer to one of their new super diesel vessels at an increased wage. He contemplated this insult with right-eous indignation.

'Diesels, indeed!' he exploded, as he carefully moved some slab toffee bars, which appeared to be growing somewhat limp from too close contact with a discreetly leaking steam pipe. He peered around him proudly in the gloom. 'I've been with the Old Lady for 30 years! Diesels! They can't touch 'er. Why, I can remember the time…'

Unobtrusively, his audience increased. One by one, the 'helpers' began to sidle into the refreshment bar. They had spent the whole afternoon behind the funnel in company with little Anthony and his Mama. He had been sitting there very quietly and tidily, and telling about the awful way the other boys carried on in choir practice…

19

The Sausage Maker's Organ

Some time ago I spent a few days with a friend who lives in a town on the outskirts of one of our larger industrial cities. It was a very go-ahead place and progress was blatantly apparent everywhere. It was in a clean air zone, and boasted a fine new main road which, if you were very alert and active, you could cross without being killed or maimed for life.

The fifteenth-century church, an architectural gem, stood in splendid isolation in the shadow of a gigantic concrete fly-over, the recent building of which had necessitated the demolishing of dozens of homes. It was, however, a very useful blot on the landscape because it allowed almost unlimited flow of diesel lorries to pass through the town unimpeded and thus pollute the air far more thoroughly and efficiently than had been possible in the unenlightened days when the houses had stood there burning their unhealthy coal fires.

A large strip of the churchyard had also been sacrificed to accommodate the fly-over and now the traffic passed so close to the church that its homely roar filled the building continuously. Indeed it almost blotted out the screams of the low-flying jet planes which, however symbolic of thrilling progress, had always tended to be just a little distracting to devotions.

Some very backward and inconsiderate members of the congregation, who didn't seem to understand that all this was progress, and imagined that they still had the right to worship in peace, had complained bitterly. The church council had told them flatly that they must realize they were living in a Brave New Age, but this didn't satisfy them at all. They replied that they weren't brave enough for the Brave New Age, and anyway they wanted to hear what they were singing about on Sundays.

One of those not affected by the new conditions was the organist. In his organ-loft he lived in a world of noise, for he controlled – or tried to – one of the most outsized organs I have ever seen.

It had been presented to the church at the turn of the century by a very generous gentleman who had made millions out of the manufacture of breakfast sausage, and who had no artistic taste whatsoever. His motto had always been 'the bigger the better' so he had ordered a five-manual instrument big and powerful enough to shatter the Royal Albert Hall.

Somehow the builders had coaxed it into the church. It bulged belligerently halfway across the chancel and overflowed into the choir vestry to such an extent that only very thin people under 5ft 5in could stand upright in the place. Pipes sprouted everywhere and the presence of a battered piano crammed into a corner gave the start- ling impression that somebody had attempted to hold a party in the engine room of a battleship.

Some of the young people of the parish had felt very strongly about the state of the vestry, and as they couldn't remove the pipes they decided that they could at least brighten the remaining visible walls. Firmly condemning the dark Victorian décor as unworthy of the church they brought in their do-it-yourself team with paint of every known and unknown hue.

The resulting catastrophe made it quite possible to imagine you were in an espresso coffee bar, if you turned your back on the pipes and got away from the engine room idea.

My friend, a member of the choir, took me along to sing at Matins, and in the unique vestry introduced me to some fellow singers. We were all rather tall and stood around bent almost double, shaking hands and looking like a venerable gathering of ancient clerics. I was told that the choir possessed some very able lady sopranos, but that I should not meet them until just before the commencement of the service. Owing to the matchbox quality of the choir vestry, they robed in the parish hall at the rear of the church. This was a temporary, corrugated iron monstrosity which had stood there for 85 years. For almost as long, its rebuilding fund had provided a good talking point on the agenda of the church council, who hadn't the slightest intention of doing anything about it.

When the girls appeared I was entranced – with their choir caps. It had always astonished me how so many attractive fashions can be created from plain black headgear and a few hair clips – but this set were really outstanding. The caps had been tortured and twisted into so many shapes on so many fantastic hairstyles that I almost imagined I was at a fashionable charity bazaar. It was quite comforting to note that my male colleagues stuck to the traditional parish church chorister's attire – veteran rusty cassocks discreetly held here and there with safety pins and topped by limp, frayed, off-white surplices with broken hangers.

At eleven o'clock the vicar herded us into the chancel to the mighty strains of the sausage-maker's organ, and I found myself shuttled to the top end of one of the magnificent black oak choir stalls. These were wonderfully carved but were not meant for relaxing in. As I sat back, an evil-looking cherub butted the back of my neck, and a creature that looked like a cross between a dragon and a certain maths mistress I once endured, kept scratching my ear.

But there was little time for relaxing anyway. The vicar had evidently decided to fight noise with noise. Throughout the service his bellow made the usual faulty loudspeakers tremble, and spurning all quiet and gentle hymns he had introduced a selection of the most rollicking, devil-may-care revivalist tunes he could lay his hands on.

We finished with honours just about even with the traffic and jet planes, but as things are going I think they'll soon have to call in the town brass band. The church must answer the challenge of progress.

20

Boiled Beef and History

My East Anglian friend always maintains that where church choirs are concerned, vicars are extremists. Either they are embarrassingly keen and are carried away with an enthusiasm which they feel entitles them to tell the choirmaster exactly how to run his choir, or else they consider the choir a necessary evil and grimly ignore it.

My friend believes that the latter attitude is often better, because if the vicar really believes he is born to direct the organist and the choir and sing every available tenor solo there is nothing much you can do about it, but if he ignores you, you can ignore him back, and practically get away with murder.

As I had sung in the village choir once or twice during holidays he considered that I was entitled to be a guest at the annual choirmen's dinner, and accordingly, one November evening, I was met from the London train by the vicar, who had kindly offered to drive me to the local tavern where the function was to be held. The vicar was very much one of the choir-ignoring type, but was always gentleman enough to endure the dinner with good grace.

The Sly Dog tavern was a delightfully medieval pile, all oak beams and death-watch beetle. In fact there were so many oak beams that I almost thought I was lost in a forest.

The meal was served punctually, and as soon as everybody had finished complaining about the seating arrangements and the fumes from the coke stove, we settled down to enjoy the boiled beef.

As is often the case, conversation died until after the sweet had arrived, and then the landlord, who was also the principal bass, rose to give his well-known speech on the history of the choir. This traced its fortunes from the eighteenth century when it was merely a small band of untrained singers tucked out of sight in the gallery, to the present day when it was a much larger band of untrained singers in full view of everybody.

We followed the landlord's forebears, who had all been choir members, through the Battle of Waterloo and on to the Crimea and the Indian Mutiny. The whole thing was brought vividly to life, but for some reason, when we got to the Boer War, the landlord seemed to lose his way and we were left hopelessly floundering with his bass grandfather at Mafeking.

Fortunately, however, one of the oldest members, who had been gently snoring since we'd charged with the Light Brigade, suddenly collapsed into his lemon meringue pie. No one cared to draw his attention to this rude behaviour, but the diversion did give the organist an opportunity of butting in smartly with grateful thanks to the speaker, and calling upon someone else to cover up with 'a few words'.

This gentleman, who obviously didn't think the drinks were moving fast enough, immediately proceeded to propose a large number of toasts. They ended with one to the vicar, who didn't enjoy boiled beef and had been missed out when they brought round the lemon meringue pie.

In a charming reply he told his annual white lie about appreciating the choir, and said he often thought what a different place the church would be if they had no choir at all. Everybody cheered frenziedly at this except the man on my left who murmured 'Shame', but I don't know whether he referred to the vicar or to a colleague opposite who had just beaten him in grabbing the last free cigarette on the table. Anyway the vicar sat down amid the continuing applause and was soon making himself a little happier increasing the tobacco smoke, which by now had settled over the room in an uncannily good imitation of a London 'pea souper'.

The organist, who could never remember what he wanted to say and had lost the old envelope bearing his notes, now neatly by-passed his turn to speak by suggesting that some members might like to 'render something'.

Unfortunately the regular alto was working overtime owing to a flu epidemic at the gasworks, and I suddenly found myself part of a quartet gathered round the piano. Out of the fog someone thrust a music copy into my hands and told me I knew the piece well. I'd never heard the thing in my life, but before I could protest we were off.

To this day I have no idea what we sang. All I remember is that at the conclusion the landlord's cat, who had been sitting on the mantelpiece, threw me a look of utter contempt and walked out. I think he was a little unfair.

Granted I may have sung a shade flat, but that piano would have flattened a Covent Garden prima donna, let alone a parish church alto.

From this point the evening wore on happily with everyone singing a solo or performing on his favourite instrument. One man, who for years had played Suppe's 'Light Cavalry' on his mouth organ, proudly varied his performance on this occasion by torturing a saw with a violin bow, and even the vicar was persuaded to murder some Gilbert and Sullivan.

Finally the Press arrived in the person of the 'local rag' reporter. Year after year he found it unnecessary to alter a single word of his account of the dinner, but of course he had always to make sure the same people *did* speak and say the same things...

21

The Great Divide

During a visit to an old friend in Dorsetshire, I was much flattered by the local vicar's pressing invitation to sing in the village church choir – until my friend explained a few things to me in a most blunt and brutal manner. Apparently, owing to the freak architecture of the church, the chancel was far more spacious than the nave, and the vicar, a hearty, blundering type, had therefore always invited visitors into the choir whether they could sing or not.

By this means he not only avoided overcrowding in the pews, but had long ago reduced the organist to a brooding introvert who had given up all hope of teaching anyone to sing. Sheer force of habit was responsible for his regular appearance in the organ loft, where he crouched Sunday by Sunday assailed by the most uproarious, unrecognizable singing, and wondered why he'd ever been born.

My friend suggested that knowing the facts I might still be surprised at the size of the choir, for a few weeks ago it had more than doubled itself overnight.

It appeared that a very advanced young organist had recently been appointed to a neighbouring church, and his first action had been to call his choir together for a friendly discussion on their future musical policy. This consisted of the organist's firmly telling the choir what they were going to do, and even more firmly condemning anyone who held different views as a stick-in-the-mud or a sort of enemy of the State.

In the circumstances the friendly discussion had turned the whole choir into enemies of the State, and they had gone off to offer their allegiance elsewhere.

Their eventual invasion of the chancel of my friend's church didn't perturb the existing choir in the least, for it was a time-honoured tradition there that no newcomers were even noticed for the first five years, and were certainly not recognized as members of the choir until they had occupied the same choir stalls for at least double that period.

Things sorted themselves out very well on the evening of my attendance. I found myself marshalled with the enemies of the State opposite the official choir, who blandly looked through us from beneath the organ. But, if the invaders were ignored, they fully reciprocated, for they took their singing time not from the organ but from their principal bass. He was a mountainous gentleman, looking uncannily like a wind-swept Shire horse, who kept thrusting a huge rubber-booted hoof into the chancel and drumming out a rhythm by kicking the side of the choir stall.

And the organist, brooding away in his loft, wondered with a vague excitement what on earth could possibly happen next. He soon knew!

At the appropriate spot the vicar announced the anthem and then, in the manner of vicars, settled back comfortably to check his sermon notes. It was not until the ensuing silence became oppressive that he looked up to face the fascinated gape of the whole choir, and realized that there was no anthem, and that somehow he had read from the previous Sunday's notices.

Quickly rising to the situation, he put away his sermon and gave out a hymn, but this misfired badly. It was from A. & M. second supplement, which was not in the books used by the congregation. The official choir had obviously never heard of it either, but it did strike a chord with some of the enemies of the State, who were stroked to victory by the rubber-booted bass, and saved the day magnificently.

The official choir recovered during the slaughtering of the next hymn, and we sang our separate ways to the point where the sermon offered some respite.

As we sat down, a choirgirl with a brazen smile and uninhibited voice handed me the parish magazine. This was an unbelievable nightmare, marked 'Price 10p or more', sporting a cover on which the names of every known parish official, long dead or just about alive, from the vicar to the retired grave-digger, were crammed into two square inches. No larger space was available after pride of place had been given to a photo of the church which looked as though it had been taken with a home-made camera by someone the worse for drink on a dirty night in 1890.

And it seemed that few of the parish officials had anything to say, for apart from the vicar's letter which explained that he would be away from the parish for the whole of August and half September, there was only an account of a jumble sale which raised £9.47p and a whist drive which hadn't taken place owing to a broken gas-main outside the village hall.

The remaining space was devoted to an advertisement from a gentleman who reckoned that he could give you a dignified funeral complete with limousines at a price far cheaper than anyone else's for miles.

The sermon was now well under way. The vicar was an ex-rugger player, and managed to remind the congregation of the fact at least once a Sunday. He was preaching about Christian unity and the team spirit. My friend said he was getting at the members of the church council who had been at loggerheads for years over the question of replacing the lectern. Apparently he tackled some parish organization from the pulpit almost every Sunday because he could speak out fearlessly and no one could answer him back. It was, however, considered very doubtful whether the choir would ever be brought down by these tactics because they never listened to the sermon anyway.

But the vicar had planned a direct approach. Bidding me farewell after the service, he added that if I came again next year I would see a great improvement in the choir. He had some ideas and was going to call the members together for a friendly discussion…

I often wonder where the enemies of the State went after that!

22

Singing in the Rain

Once, in the days when I still had a touching faith in the existence of the English summer, I holidayed in a small village in the shadow of the White Horse hills of Berkshire.

As usual, I worked my way into the local church choir, and thus added another chapter to my appalling musical background.

The vicar, a pale and eager young man, said he was only too pleased to welcome anyone – just anyone – who was willing to have a go in the choir, no matter what kind of voice they had – as so many members were on holiday enjoying the rain somewhere else.

He explained that on this particular Sunday a special opening ceremony had been arranged for the new children's recreation ground at the rear of the church. A strong choir was needed to lead the important parish officials in the singing of three of the only six hymns which they all vaguely knew.

At 5.30 in the afternoon the choir, consisting of about 20 men, boys and girls, processed out of the vestry and through the jungle of the graveyard to the new recreation ground.

Of course, the usual fine refreshing summer deluge was doing its best, and so that we should not get too refreshed we were all grouped under an ancient oak tree with the important parish officials, while members of the public were left high – but hardly dry – to do what they could with sunshades and newspapers.

Meanwhile the vicar took up his position on a kind of dais near the new, gaily painted slide, down which the rain was cascading like a joyous mountain waterfall.

Our tree broke the force of the deluge, and only gentle streams of dirty water from the branches filtered through on most of the choir. I was on the end of the row, however, and could hardly get under the tree at all, but it didn't matter much because the branch nearest me was dead and supported no foliage anyway.

We sang the first hymn, 'All things bright and beautiful', and then the vicar, still very eager, commenced his speech. It started very well, and I think he was hitting many nails firmly on the head, but I must admit that my attention wandered a little as I noticed the row of choir-girls in front of me growing shorter and shorter as their high heels sank deeper and deeper in the mud.

Then, as the vicar waxed more eloquent, he won my attention again. He beamed at his congregation and talked about the sunshine that their children brought into their lives. And the man next to me, his eyes fixed in glassy attention, discreetly cuffed the top choirboy who was discreetly splashing mud all over a junior choirgirl's white socks.

Finally the vicar pointed dramatically in the direction of the White Horse hills, which were completely obliterated in rain and clouds, and said how splendid it was that the village children could now play in this spot within the sight of one of the most beautiful views in the British Isles.

So persuasive was he that I found myself straining my eyes in the direction of his outflung hand, but as visibility was down to a few yards all I could make out was a ramshackle tavern called The Artichoke, which sprawled tipsily by the side of an evil-smelling duck pond.

The most important of the important parish officials now came forward with his wife to say his little piece, and cut a pink ribbon which was stretched across the main entrance of the ground. He was a small man who had probably been pushed into public life against his will by his wife, a very forceful and determined-looking woman. Anyway his heart wasn't in this bit of public life, for he looked really pitiful as he dejectedly declared how very happy he was to be present.

To make matters worse, he had forgotten his scissors, and there was a delay while someone untied the ribbon from the fence, while his wife regarded him in a most unfriendly way.

Finally the choir came into their own again, and the congregation cheered themselves up, with the raucous singing of two more popular hymns.

These hymns had no bearing whatsoever on the occasion and indeed even contradicted each other. But, with few exceptions, it is the composers of the tunes, not the writers of the words, which have made our English hymns famous. The average Englishman will happily sing any words to a good tune.

We now returned to the church for Evensong, and it struck me that the locals must have been quite used to the blessings of continual rain, because no one in the choir seemed in the least perturbed as we squelched into the choir stalls to open the service with 'The radiant morn has passed away'. I think they even considered the whole proceedings a little tame, for during the sermon the man next to me recalled wistfully the occasion when they had sung at the opening of the new almshouses. There had been a thunderstorm then, and the place had been struck by lightning.

After the service the vicar seemed to sense that I wasn't so keen on water as were his flock, and realizing that I was faced with a goodish walk to my lodgings he said that we'd take a short cut to the vicarage and he'd lend me an umbrella. The short cut was twice as far as the normal way and involved negotiating a field that had turned itself into a lake.

By the time we reached the vicarage it didn't much matter whether I had an umbrella or not. However, I opened it, and at that moment the sun burst through the clouds like a huge glowing face. It grinned at me wickedly.

23

A Place for Everything

I was early for Evensong at the village church where I'd been invited to join the choir during a summer holiday weekend. The only other person to be seen was a little man in a black suit with a thick watch chain who appeared to be running in and out of the pews at a furious rate, sweeping up armfuls of hymn books and tumbling them into a pew just inside the church door.

'People just do not care these days,' he declared, cannoning into me and spilling books amongst the flowers around the font. 'They leave their hymn books all over the place after every service – forget their hats and umbrellas all the time – I even found three tins of cat food last week. Goodness knows what their houses are like if they never put anything away.' He added an umbrella, a pair of gloves, a pink teddy bear and a bottle of aspirin to a large pile in a cardboard box. 'There'll be enough here to stock a whole stall at the next jumble sale,' he forecast, 'there always is.'

He looked towards the chancel. 'And as for the choir – come and have a look.' He led me up the chancel at a brisk trot. 'Look!' I saw his point. Hymn books, Psalters and sheet music and a smattering of parish magazines lay in gay abandon all over the splendid eighteenth-century choir stalls. My guide advanced on a particularly large and ragged pile of music tottering at the end of one of the stalls. 'Next thing we know, they'll be falling all over the place,' he said. 'Fred – er, he's the organist – really must do something about this. He must have a go at that choir lot…'

As he spoke, a teenaged choirgirl appeared from the vestry in the process of donning a voluminous choir gown and veiling a violet and pink T-shirt which bore an outsized advertisement for someone's original Olde English beer. 'Don't you move those, Charlie,' she warned. 'You know what happens when you do that. At the last minute before the service Fred goes to give 'em out and can't find 'em, and then he starts shouting at me and I start shouting back – and you know how some of them in the congregation complain when they hear us shouting in the vestry. No end of a fuss. You'd better leave 'em alone. Then Fred knows where to find 'em.'

'Why does he shout at you?' I said.

'I'm the choir librarian,' she said, moving the books about haphazardly. 'I'm supposed to know where all the music is when Fred wants it.'

'Quite a job, I imagine,' I said.

'Oh, you get to know where everything is,' she assured me easily, 'as long as Charlie doesn't keep on moving it.'

'I don't know what we're coming to,' exploded Charlie, and trotted back down the nave to give out the hymn books again as members of the congregation started to arrive.

The choirgirl now took me into the vestry and deposited me amongst the small band of choir men of various ages, who were very friendly and seemed eager to know everything about me including where I was born, if I was married, and where I usually fished. I explained that I didn't fish, and this seemed to disconcert them somewhat, and they drifted away leaving me with the vicar, who had just arrived and had indeed earlier invited me into the choir as I stood admiring his dahlias on leaving the station the previous evening. He was a large, middle-aged, beaming, untidy man with battered black shoes with turned-up toes. He flopped a wad of pencil-written notes on top of the piano, swept off his jacket and knocked them all over the floor. He bundled himself into a rusty black cassock while I retrieved his notes. 'Thanks,' he puffed, screwing them all together into his pocket. 'Sermon notes. Never look at them but always have to have them with me.' He swept out his arm, knocking someone's check cap off the piano. 'No room to put anything in here, I'm afraid.' He surveyed three long Victorian school forms and two garden chairs all weighted down with books, sheet music, cassocks and surplices and boxes of half-spent candles. 'Have to be careful though. We did have a tidy-up some years ago but there was an awful row. The choir reckoned they couldn't find anything afterwards. Still looking for Fred's spare reading glasses, I believe.'

Right on time the vicar hustled us all into Evensong, beamed at the congregation and said hello, everyone, what a glorious day it had been and announced the first hymn. If, as in this case, Fred had not found time to give out the music, the idea seemed to be to grab a hymn book, Psalter and copy of the anthem from the scattered random piles as you filed into the choir stalls, and obviously these choristers were seasoned experts. As a newcomer, however, I was rather at a disadvantage and found myself with three Psalters, two out-of-date parish magazines and no hymn book, so I missed the first verse, but shortly I was lucky enough to trip over a secluded Ancient and Modern that seemed to have got itself wedged behind two kneelers, so I caught up with everyone at the second verse of the hymn. Thereafter things were easy. I knew the anthem – a short, simple one by Attwood – which we sang through twice. The man next to me, who said his name was Winston, explained that they always sang Attwood anthems through twice because Attwood composed such short anthems it was hardly worth the vicar announcing them and the congregation sitting down to hear them if they were only sung through once…

As far as the congregation were concerned it was hard to know what they thought about Attwood because all their faces wore that inscrutable expression that the faces of congregations do wear when the choir is ploughing through an anthem, or the vicar has preached for more than five minutes, or an appeal for cash is being bade to restore the organ or level off the gravestones in the churchyard.

When, in fact, we arrived at the sermon, it did last considerably longer than five minutes and Winston, who knew about Attwood, having perused the parish magazine, punctuating his reading with exclamations such as 'Rubbish!' 'The man's an idiot!' and 'Waste of paper!', leaned across to me and whispered harshly, 'Course,

Attwood was organist at St Paul's Cathedral at the beginning of the nineteenth century, you know, and they had an awful choir there then. They couldn't do the big stuff.' He thought for a moment. 'I wonder if Attwood was like Fred – good on the organ but no good running the choir. I bet he was like Fred.' He thought again. 'Tell you what, though, I bet he saw to it that his choir at least had pegs to hang their cassocks on. We've only got three pegs and two nails in the wall here. Fred's always going to do something about it but never does. I bet Attwood differed from Fred there.' Further speculation about the probable similarities and dissimilarities between Thomas Attwood and Fred were halted by a comfortable-looking choir lady at the end of the row, who was discreetly knitting what looked like a very elaborate dishcloth. She had dropped her ball of wool, which had rolled under Winston's seat. With surprising agility – for he was a bulky elderly man – Winston plunged sideways and under the choir stall whence started to appear all kinds of unexpected articles – an ancient shoe, a dog's rubber bone, a broken umbrella and two or three liquorice allsorts packets. 'It's gone right to the back behind a lot of other stuff,' came his muffled voice as he disappeared further under the seat. As the sermon ended and the vicar announced the final hymn, Winston, his face red and triumphant, appeared again, and he arose, gallantly handing a cobwebbed, dust-covered ball of wool to its owner.

In the vestry after the service it became obvious that the little man in the black suit, who had earlier introduced me to the church's untidiness problem, and who

I learned was the vicar's warden, had decided to make a move about the situation, starting with the choir. Before anyone could throw off their robes and escape, he had stationed himself in the doorway and announced that he wanted a word. And by the time Fred had finished his voluntary the warden had unburdened himself of his thoughts on the subjects of slackness, lack of responsibility, absence of pride in one's work, turning a blind eye and downright sordid squalor, and gone off to supper much relieved and greatly satisfied with the knowledge of an important job well done. And the choir had happily dispersed as usual, quite unaware that any job had been done at all.

I waited in the empty vestry for Fred, who had invited me to supper. He bustled in, dropping his gown over the back of a chair from which it slowly slid to the floor. 'What did he want?' he asked. 'I saw him come into the vestry and he looked more foul tempered than usual.'

'The vicar's warden, you mean?' I asked. 'Yes, he gave us a little talk about tidiness.'

'Can't understand him,' mused Fred. 'Always on about that. Seems to have some fixation. You see, he's retired now and hasn't got much to do. I wish he'd get a part-time job or something.'

'He says the choir vestry's a rubbish tip,' I said.

Fred looked around his domain. 'Well, it's not all that tidy, I suppose, but it's not bad.' He moved various piles of books and music to slightly different positions, studied them and moved them back again. 'We know where everything is,' he justified, 'old Psalters there, new ones here and here, two dozen old edition Ancient and Mod-

erns in the corner here, spare cassocks under here, surplices to be mended up here, pictures of 25 years of choir
outings to Margate behind the table here. Mendelssohn's
Elijah' – his eye searched and found half-a-dozen copies
propping up an ancient record chest – 'yes, Elijah over
here, and the anthem I composed last year to celebrate
my 40 years as organist here.' Again his eye searched,
but this time didn't find. 'Here, where have they put it?
Here! I say!' He started rummaging wildly among the
chaos. Piles of books tumbled, cassocks and surplices
tangled round his feet. He attempted to move the piano
and from its lid someone's abandoned half cup of coffee
emptied down his tie…

I had an idea. 'Just a minute,' I called, as I went quickly
back to the choir stalls and crouched and looked under
Winston's seat. I dragged out again the articles he had
tidied back after retrieving the ball of wool. A little further
back my fingers touched a dusty package. I wondered…

'Yes, this is it,' beamed Fred, abandoning a half-sorted
pile of music in the middle of the floor. 'Where did you
find them? Under the choir stalls! Now that's not a bad
idea. We could have a lot of extra storage space there.
Yes, we could get tons of stuff under the seats. What a
good idea.'

I wonder if the vicar's warden has examined the choir
stalls lately?